VIEWPOINT

WORKBOOK 2A

MICHAEL MCCARTHY

JEANNE MCCARTEN

HELEN SANDIFORD

CAMBRIDGE
UNIVERSITY PRESS

CAMBRIDGE
UNIVERSITY PRESS

University Printing House, Cambridge CB2 8BS, United Kingdom

One Liberty Plaza, 20th Floor, New York, NY 10006, USA

477 Williamstown Road, Port Melbourne, VIC 3207, Australia

314–321, 3rd Floor, Plot 3, Splendor Forum, Jasola District Centre, New Delhi – 110025, India

103 Penang Road, #05-06/07, Visioncrest Commercial, Singapore 238467

Cambridge University Press is part of the University of Cambridge.

It furthers the University's mission by disseminating knowledge in the pursuit of education, learning and research at the highest international levels of excellence.

www.cambridge.org
Information on this title: www.cambridge.org/9781107572058

© Cambridge University Press 2015

First published 2015

20 19 18 17 16 15 14 13 12 11 10

Printed in Poland by Opolgraf

A catalog record for this publication is available from the British Library.

ISBN 978-0-521-13189-6 Student's Book
ISBN 978-1-107-60154-3 Student's Book A
ISBN 978-1-107-60155-0 Student's Book B
ISBN 978-1-107-60631-9 Workbook
ISBN 978-1-107-57213-3 Workbook B
ISBN 978-1-107-60156-7 Teacher's Edition with Assessment Audio CD/CD-ROM
ISBN 978-1-107-66132-5 Class Audio CDs (4)
ISBN 978-1-107-67577-3 Presentation Plus
ISBN 978-1-107-56841-9 Student's Book with Updated Online Workbook
ISBN 978-1-107-56846-4 Student's Book with Updated Online Workbook A
ISBN 978-1-107-56849-5 Student's Book with Updated Online Workbook B
ISBN 978-1-107-56808-2 Student's Book with Online Course (includes Online Workbook)
ISBN 978-1-107-56809-9 Student's Book with Online Course (includes Online Workbook) A
ISBN 978-1-107-56810-5 Student's Book with Online Course (includes Online Workbook) B

Additional resources for this publication at www.cambridge.org/viewpoint

Contents

A great read

Lesson A Grammar Avoiding repetition 1

A Complete the sentences with the words in the box. Use each word at least once.

am	did	do	doesn't	haven't

1. I'm following in my siblings' footsteps. They're working hard for their degrees, and now I _____ , too.
2. My coworker is thinking about getting a different job – as I _____ . We both think it's time for a career change.
3. I've always loved new experiences and new adventures, but my best friend _____ . She prefers to stay at home and read about other people's adventures.
4. Since I had children, I haven't taken many risks in my life. My friends _____ , either – we're all comfortable with how our lives are right now.
5. I want to plan a trip to go whitewater rafting next year – my friends _____ , too. I really hope the plan works out, and I know they _____ , too.
6. I've always dreamed of becoming a professional musician. When he was younger, my brother _____ , too, but he ended up becoming a lawyer. These days, he only plays his guitar for his own enjoyment.

B Complete the sentences with auxiliary verbs.

1. My classmates think it's a good idea to get some work experience before they graduate. I _____ , too.
2. My sister and I decided to travel all over Europe by train last fall. She worked extra hours before our vacation so we'd have enough money. I _____ , too.
3. Have you seen the new exhibit at the museum? I haven't seen it yet, but my friend _____ . She said it's amazing.
4. Some of my classmates are struggling to complete their required courses for graduation – they're finding it tough, as I _____ .
5. I wanted to go hiking yesterday, but my friend _____ . I'm going to ask my cousin to hike with me today. I don't know if he likes hiking. Hopefully he _____ .
6. My parents have applied for a visa to emigrate to Australia, but I _____ . They really want to go soon, but I _____ . I have too many friends here.

About you **C** Compare yourself with a friend or family member. How are your interests and daily lives the same or different?

For example: *I've done a lot of traveling around the world, but my brother hasn't.*

_____

_____

_____

_____

_____

Lesson B Vocabulary Favorite books

A Read the blog post. Circle the best option to complete the sentences.

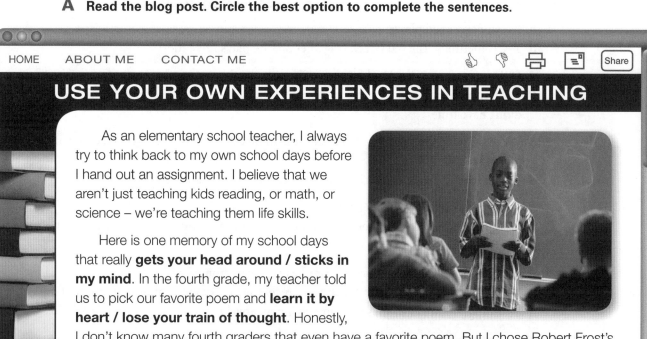

USE YOUR OWN EXPERIENCES IN TEACHING

As an elementary school teacher, I always try to think back to my own school days before I hand out an assignment. I believe that we aren't just teaching kids reading, or math, or science – we're teaching them life skills.

Here is one memory of my school days that really **gets your head around / sticks in my mind**. In the fourth grade, my teacher told us to pick our favorite poem and **learn it by heart / lose your train of thought**. Honestly, I don't know many fourth graders that even have a favorite poem. But I chose Robert Frost's *Birches*, which is really long. There I was, ready to recite the poem, and all of a sudden I just froze. **It was on the tip of my tongue / It was beyond me**, but I just couldn't remember how it started. Eventually I remembered and recited the whole poem. And I've remembered it ever since. I can recite that poem today **come to grips with / off the top of my head**.

I know my students don't really **see the point / come to mind** of reciting poetry, especially if they **can't make head or tails of / stick in their mind** what they are saying. However, I feel like I really **learned by heart / got something out of** that activity when I was in school. At the time, I was terrified, but with each new poem I recited, I gained a bit more confidence.

It may have been a rough start, but my fourth grade teacher unwittingly paved the way for my career. Even when I **lose my train of thought / see the point**, I have no fear standing in front of a class now.

About you

B Complete the sentences with your own ideas.

1. It's beyond me why _____ .
2. Something that really sticks in my mind is _____ .
3. _____ always comes to mind when I think about my childhood.
4. I can't really see the point of _____ .
5. One thing I can't come to grips with is _____ .
6. It's easy to lose your train of thought when _____ .
7. It's very rewarding when you can get your head around _____ .
8. I've never learned _____ by heart.
9. _____ is something that I can never make heads or tails of.
10. Whenever I answer a question off the top of my head without thinking about it, _____ .

Lesson B Grammar Avoiding repetition 2

A Read the conversations. Delete words or replace them with *one / ones*, where possible, to avoid repetition. Sometimes more than one answer is possible.

1. *A* Do you ever read plays?

   B Yes, sometimes. The old Greek tragedies are the plays I like most.

2. *A* Did you read *To Kill a Mockingbird* in English class?

   B No, our professor said we were supposed to read *To Kill a Mockingbird*, but then we didn't have time.

3. *A* We're studying the poetry of Pablo Neruda in literature class. Have you read any of his poetry?

   B Yeah. I love it. I memorized his poetry to recite in my poetry class once.

4. *A* Do you ever read gossip magazines?

   B Well, I prefer not to read them, but sometimes if I'm waiting at the doctor's office I might look at a gossip magazine.

5. *A* My English teacher writes novels. Her last two were published.

   B Yes, I know her novels. I think her more recent novel is much better than her first novel.

   A Yeah, I agree. Actually, she's working on a new novel now.

B Read the conversation. Delete words or replace them with *one / ones*, where possible, to avoid repetition. Sometimes more than one answer is possible.

A I need something to read. Have you read anything good lately?

B Well, I've been reading a lot of crime novels lately. You can borrow a crime novel if you like. Do you want to borrow a crime novel?

A Thanks, but I don't like to read books about murders. I generally prefer not to read books about murders, or I get nightmares.

B OK. How about a classic like *Great Expectations*?

A Yeah, that sounds good. I've never read that classic, and I've always wanted to read that novel.

B We read it in our literature class a few years ago. Well, actually, we were supposed to read it, but I watched the movie instead.

A You did? That's funny. There are so many movies of the classics nowadays. But usually I don't watch the movie until after I've read the book, or at least I try not to watch the movie until I've read the book. Usually the books are better.

B Yeah. I have to say I usually prefer the movie. Anyway, take *Great Expectations*. Or I have some Shakespeare plays, too. I think I have most of his plays. Here, take that Shakespeare play, *Romeo and Juliet*, or *Hamlet*. You can borrow both plays if you like. I hope *Hamlet* doesn't give you nightmares, though!

A OK. Thanks.

About you **C** What kinds of books do you read? Who is your favorite author? Do you like all of his or her books? Has your taste in books changed over the years?

_____

_____

_____

Lesson C   Conversation strategies

A Complete the conversation. Use the verbs in the box and add the auxiliary verbs *do* or *does* to add emphasis.

appreciate	feel	make	need	think

Tamara   So, Carolina, how do you like your e-reader?

Carolina   Well, I have to say I _____¹ not having to carry books anymore. And I have much more room in my purse, that's for sure.

Tamara   I know. I like mine, too. But it _____² a bit strange, you know, not turning the pages.

Carolina   Is yours an older one? Like, is it in black and white? This one's in color, and it _____³ a difference – especially if you're reading magazines and stuff.

Tamara   Oh, yeah, I bet. I _____⁴ a new one, actually. But you know what I like best? If I run out of things to read when I'm traveling, I can just download something.

Carolina   I know. I have to say though, I haven't figured out all the functions on it yet. I _____⁵ they could be easier to navigate. Like, I deleted a book the other day when I was just trying to bookmark something.

Tamara   You'll get used to it soon enough.

B Complete the conversation with *if so* or *if not*.

Teacher   OK, class, good luck with your papers, and remember, if you quote from someone's work, the references must be accurate. _____¹ , you'll be penalized and get a lower grade.

Student   Um, can I reference Internet blogs in my paper? And _____² , what is the correct way to do that?

Teacher   You may, but in my view simply restating one blogger's ideas is a weak, _____³ pointless thing to do. I want to see evidence that you have consulted real authorities. As to the second question, do you have the college style guide? _____⁴ , you'll find all referencing information there. _____⁵ , you can access it on my website.

About you

C Complete the conversations with *if so, if not,* or write the auxiliary verbs *do* or *does* to add emphasis where possible. Then answer with your own information.

1. *A* Do you use social media sites a lot? And _____ , what do you use them for?

   B Yes, I _____ spend a lot of time on social media sites, catching up with news. And I read a lot of blogs, too. Blogs really _____ give everyone a chance to express their point of view.

   _____

2. *A* My friend just submitted a story to a publisher. She's hoping they'll publish it but _____ , she'll have to find another way to get it published. Any thoughts?

   B Well, she could publish it herself online. I mean it _____ take a little effort, but it works for some authors.

   _____

Lesson D Reading Dallas Poetry Slam – FAQs

A **Prepare What do you know about poetry slams? Check the statement you think is true. Then read the website and check your answer.**

    1. They are non-competitive. _____
    2. They are for professional writers only. _____
    3. They combine the talent for writing poetry and performing. _____

Home   Events   Sign-up   **FAQ**   Contact Us

Dallas POETRY SLAM – FAQs[1]

1 What is poetry slam?
Simply put, poetry slam is the competitive art of performance poetry. It puts a dual emphasis on writing and performance, encouraging poets to focus on what they're saying and how they're saying it.

2 What is a poetry slam?
A poetry slam is a competitive event in which poets perform their work and are judged by members of the audience. Typically, the host or another organizer selects the judges, who are instructed to give numerical scores (on a 0 to 10 or 1 to 10 scale) based on the poets' content and performance.

3 Who gets to participate?
Slams are open to everyone who wishes to sign up and can get into the venue. Though everyone who signs up has the opportunity to read in the first round, the lineup for subsequent rounds is determined by the judges' scores. In other words, the judges vote for which poets they want to see more work from.

4 What are the rules?
Each poem must be of the poet's own construction. Each poet gets three minutes (plus a 10-second grace period) to read one poem. If the poet goes over time, points will be deducted from the total score. The poet may not use props, costumes, or musical instruments. Of the scores the poet receives from the five judges, the high and low scores are dropped, and the middle three are added together, giving the poet a total score of 0–30.

5 How does it differ from an open mike[2] reading?
Slam is engineered for the audience, whereas a number of open mike readings are engineered as a support network for poets. Slam is designed for the audience to react vocally and openly to all aspects of the show, including the poet's performance, the judges' scores, and the host's banter.

6 What can the audience do?
The official MC spiel of Poetry Slam, Inc., encourages the audience to respond to the poets or the judges in any way they see fit, and most slams have adopted that guideline. Audiences can boo or cheer at the conclusion of a poem, or even during a poem.

7 What kind of poetry is read at slams?
Depends on the venue, depends on the poets, depends on the slam. One of the best things about poetry slam is the range of poets it attracts. You'll find a diverse range of work within slam, including heartfelt love poetry, searing social commentary, uproarious comic routines, and bittersweet personal confessional pieces. Poets are free to do work in any style on any subject.

8 How do I win a poetry slam?
Winning a poetry slam requires some measure of skill and a huge dose of luck. The judges' tastes, the audience's reactions, and the poets' performances all shape a slam event, and what wins one week might not get a poet into the second round the next week. There's no formula for winning a slam, although you become a stronger poet and performer the same way you get to Carnegie Hall — practice, practice, practice.

SOURCE: Poetry Slam, Inc.
[1]*FAQs* frequently asked questions
[2]*open mike* a live show where audience members get up on stage, take the mike (= microphone), and perform

B Read for main ideas Choose the correct option to complete the sentences. Write a, b, or c.

1. In order to win a poetry slam, poets have to focus on _____ .
   a. their poetry writing skills
   b. the delivery of their poem
   c. both a and b
2. The judges at a poetry slam are chosen by _____ .
   a. the audience
   b. an event official
   c. the poets
3. All participants at a poetry slam have to _____ .
   a. read a number of poems
   b. read their own poem
   c. read classic poetry
4. A slam is different from an open mike because _____ .
   a. an open mike event focuses on entertaining the audience
   b. a slam is designed to provide support for young poets
   c. the audience's reaction is what matters most
5. At a slam, audience members _____ .
   a. might show support and cheer for the performers
   b. are asked to calm down if they react too loudly
   c. both a and b
6. One of the unique things about poetry slams is _____ .
   a. that the audience can determine the theme for the event
   b. all of the poems for an event focus on one topic
   c. it includes many different types of poetry
7. To win poetry slams, you need _____ .
   a. to be a consistently strong performer
   b. to gauge the audience's reaction, amongs other things
   c. nothing more than a big dose of luck

C Read for detail Are the sentences true or false, or is the information not given on the webpage? Write T, F, or NG. Correct the false sentences.

1. At a poetry slam, poets receive a score for their performance. _____
2. The performers at a poetry slam have all been invited to participate. _____
3. Poetry slams started 10 years ago. _____
4. A poet can read a poem that he / she did not write. _____
5. Performers get penalized for spending too much time on one poem. _____
6. A poet can use any items during the performance to enhance their reading. _____
7. Poetry slams are becoming more popular than open mike readings. _____
8. Poems on political issues are not allowed at poetry slams. _____

About you

D React Answer the questions with your own opinions.

1. Would you like to go to a poetry slam? Why?

   _____

   _____

2. What characteristics do you think a person needs to be successful at a poetry slam?

   _____

   _____

Writing A book review

A Underline the linked adjectives in the book review.

A dark yet thrilling novel, Fyodor Dostoevsky's *Crime and Punishment* focuses on the psychological aspects of murder. Published in 1866, the novel describes how the main character, Raskolnikov, plans and executes a murder and deals with the resulting guilt. Raskolnikov is a thoughtful though arrogant character. His arrogance prompts him to commit a terrible, even brutal, crime to prove his superiority.

Throughout the novel, Dostoevsky builds a tense, dramatic chain of events by simultaneously describing the criminal investigation and Raskolnikov's psychological state. His internal suffering eventually comes to an unpredictable though perhaps realistic resolution. Readers of *Crime and Punishment* may find it a disturbing, if not depressing, work. However, it does provide the reader with an insight into the innermost thoughts of a criminal. As a whole, it is considered one of the best examples of nineteenth century Russian literature.

B Circle the best option to complete the sentences from a review of *Crime and Punishment*.

1. *Crime and Punishment* is a long **yet / or even** action-packed novel, filled with a number of unexpected events.
2. At the beginning of the book, we see a cold **, / yet** detached young man planning a crime he feels he has every right to commit.
3. After committing the crime, his confused **and / if** desperate actions reflect his guilt about the murder.
4. Things start to turn against him when he rants about the crime to a concerned **yet / if not** suspicious official.
5. The official's clever, **even / but** insightful plan is to make Raskolnikov worry so much about being caught that he eventually confesses.
6. A nervous **but / and** anxious Raskolnikov eventually confesses to his crime.

C Editing Correct the mistakes in the coordinated adjectives, but do not use *and*.
More than one answer is possible. One sentence is correct.

1. Dostoevsky's novels are complex yet difficult.
2. His work has often been described as thought-provoking philosophical.
3. The vocabulary in the book is rich, at times obscure.
4. It forces us to ask some difficult if not impossible questions about ourselves.
5. Readers may find the initial plot development slow, boring.
6. For me, reading a Dostoevsky novel is an intriguing though fascinating experience.
7. However, his novels can leave the reader feeling saddened but depressed.

D Think of a book you have enjoyed that has memorable characters. Write a review evaluating both the story and the characters. Check your work for errors.

Listening extra A young novelist

A Imagine you want to become a published author. Which three things would you try to do?

_____ Start by writing a blog on the Internet.

_____ Try to publish a story in a school or student newspaper.

_____ Attend a writer's workshop.

_____ Perform at a poetry slam.

_____ Self-publish an e-book.

_____ Try to get accepted to a writers' conference.

_____ Take a creative writing class.

_____ Share your ideas for a book with your friends.

_____ Ask established authors to edit your work.

B Listen to the radio interview with Rebecca Jackson. Check (✔) the things from Exercise A that she tried doing to get published.

C Listen again. Are the sentences true or false? Write T or F.

1. *2050* is Rebecca's first novel. _____
2. Rebecca's professor did not have any advice for aspiring writers. _____
3. Rebecca received an "A" in her creative writing class. _____
4. Despite her setbacks, Rebecca's urge to communicate with people kept her motivated. _____
5. Rebecca's parents thought it was a good idea for her to take a year off school. _____
6. Rebecca heard about self-published e-books at a poetry slam event. _____

D Listen again and complete the sentences.

1. Rebecca is _____ years old.
2. She took a creative writing class during her _____ year in college.
3. Her short story was rejected from the _____ _____ .
4. Rebecca loved the idea of e-books because she wouldn't have to contend with large, _____ publishers.
5. Jenny Davis, the main character in *2050,* is a shy _____ young woman.
6. The host of the radio show describes the main character as soft-spoken yet rather _____ .

About you

E Answer the questions with your own opinions.

1. If you wanted to publish a book, would you publish it yourself, or would you try to get it published by a big publisher? Why?

_____

_____

2. Will the ability for people to publish their own e-books mean more great books getting published, or will it mean more uninteresting books by bad authors?

_____

_____

Now complete the *Unit 1 Progress chart* on page 98.

Technology

Lesson A Grammar Adding information to nouns

A Replace the underlined relative clauses with other types of phrases. Sometimes more than one answer is possible.

ONLINE PRIVACY: A Generational Divide

By Dr. Jane Thomas

Recently I had my sociology class read an article about online privacy and security.

In my opinion, online privacy is a topic that should be taken[1] very seriously. Therefore I devoted an entire class period to the topic. I thought students would be surprised to discover how advertisers create ads for each consumer that are based on data[2] they have collected[3] from previous purchases or product searches. I anticipated that they would be disturbed to learn about programs that are designed to search[4] for keywords in your emails in order to target advertising. However, to my surprise, the students who are in my class[5] did not seem at all concerned about online privacy and security. In fact, some students who were no doubt hoping to reassure me[6] noted that it is sometimes beneficial to see advertisements that are directly targeted[7] to their needs and interests. Many of my students said

that adjusting the settings which are on their account[8] provides a sense of security.

When I asked them how they would feel about random people who live around the world[9] viewing all their photos and other personal information on social networking sites, many of them reported that this idea was not something that they need to worry about[10]. For my students, personal information is something that can be shared[11]. By the end of the class, I concluded that my students' views on online security were yet another example of the generational divide that exists[12] between those who grew up with technology and those who didn't.

1. _to be taken_
2. _____
3. _____
4. _____

5. _____
6. _____
7. _____
8. _____

9. _____
10. _____
11. _____
12. _____

About you

B Complete the questions with correct forms of the verbs given. Then answer the questions. Give reasons for your answers.

1. What do you think about websites _____ (display) ads for items _____ (base) on similar items you have looked at online?

2. Do you think email messages _____ (provide) coupons based on your recent purchases are something _____ (welcome), or are they an invasion of privacy _____ (condemn)?

3. Are you concerned about social networking sites _____ (program) to share your personal information with advertisers? Why or why not?

Lesson B Vocabulary Compound adjectives

A Complete the blog post with the expressions in the box. There is one extra expression.

air-conditioned	energy-efficient	home-cooked	self-cleaning
climate-controlled	high-speed	last-minute	solar-powered

HOME   MY TRAVELS   ABOUT ME   CONTACT ME

Do you want to get away from it all? GO LOW-TECH!

Goodbye vacation I'm sure you've had this same experience: You plan a vacation, but you end up working during your time off. You arrive to find yourself stuck in an _____[1] room, instead of enjoying the fresh air and tropical temperatures on the beach. You feel obligated to answer emails because you have access to the hotel's _____[2] Internet. And just when you finally think you are free, your boss makes a _____[3] request! Goodbye vacation! Sound familiar?

Time to go low-tech! I have worked during one too many vacations. So this year, I decided to go completely low-tech. I stayed in a bungalow on the beach. There was no Internet or cell service. I went in the summer, but the room was _____[4] with the sea breezes through the open windows. The water heater for the shower was _____[5], which is perfect for a place that is sunny most of the year. These are true examples of _____[6] accommodations!

I ate delicious _____[7] meals prepared by the owners. They were fantastic! So, next time you are planning a vacation, go low-tech, and get away from it all.

B Complete the discussion with the expressions in the box. There is one extra expression.

carbon-neutral	custom-built	human-like	labor-saving	last-minute

Host OK. Let's take some questions from the audience. Yes, sir, what's your question?

Man Um, is it your intention to create a robot that not only looks like a regular person, but is also _____[1] in other ways?

Professor Well, at this point, we're trying to make certain jobs less time-consuming, so we see robots as _____[2] devices. We don't imagine they'll have more caring human qualities.

Woman I'd like to ask, when you assemble robots, are they always _____[3] for particular customers? I mean, do people order them for their own purposes?

Professor It depends on the customer. We usually try to tackle several problems at once.

Woman And how about the cost of running a robot? Do they use a lot of energy?

Professor Actually, we've also been working on an eco-friendly robot that is _____[4].

About you **C** Imagine you could have a custom-built robot. What would it be like? Would it be human-like? Energy-efficient? What labor-saving chores would it do? Write a paragraph.

Lesson B Grammar Combining ideas

A Complete the article with the conjunctions *both . . . and, either . . . or, neither . . . nor,* and *not only . . . but also.* Sometimes there is more than one correct answer.

MASDAR CITY

In 2008, construction began on the first sustainable city in the world, known as Masdar City. Located 11 miles (17 kilometers) outside of Abu Dhabi in the United Arab Emirates, Masdar City is designed to be an eco-friendly urban environment. The city depends _____not only_____[1] on renewable energy sources, _____[2] aims to create a zero-waste ecology. Consequently, _____[3] gas-powered cars _____[4] equipment that uses fossil fuels are permitted within the city limits. City planners designed the city to provide two easy forms of transportation. Residents can _____[5] walk _____[6] take driverless electric vehicles all around this modern landscape. Masdar City has given city planners around the globe _____[7] a model for a high-tech, sustainable city _____[8] new insights into creating energy-efficient living spaces.

B Rewrite the sentences using the conjunctions in parentheses.

1. Masdar City relies on technological innovation. It also draws on traditional Arabic architecture. (not only . . . but also) _Masdar City not only relies on technological innovation, but it also draws on traditional Arabic architecture_ .

2. In Masdar City, solar power will be used to generate energy. Wind farms will also be used. (both . . . and) _____ _____ .

3. Biological waste will not be thrown away. Industrial waste will also not be thrown away. (neither . . . nor) _____ _____ .

4. The completion of Masdar City will be in 2020. It might be in 2025. (either . . . or) _____ _____ .

5. The walls surrounding the city were designed to keep out gas-powered cars. They were also designed for protection from the hot, desert winds. (not only . . . but also) _____ _____ .

6. Clean-tech companies are expected to occupy some of the city's buildings. Major research institutes are also expected to occupy some of the buildings. (both . . . and) _____ _____ .

7. According to the plans, wastewater will be used for crop irrigation. It could also be used to maintain the city's parks. (either . . . or) _____ _____ .

About you

C Describe your ideal city. What would make it more innovative and high-tech than where you live now? Use conjunctions to explain your ideas.

_____
_____
_____

Lesson C   Conversation strategies

A **Circle the best options to complete the conversation.**

Victoria   Sorry I'm late. I was walking out the door when Sara called. She got into a car accident a few hours ago.

Yarah   Oh, no! Really? Is she OK?

Victoria   Yeah. Thankfully, she's fine and no one else was involved. **Predictably / Invariably**, she was talking on her hands-free headset and driving at the same time. She **ideally / evidently** got distracted and hit a tree on the side of the road.

Yarah   You're kidding! I've told her a million times it's not a good idea to drive and talk on the phone at the same time. Even if she is wearing her headset.

Victoria   I know. I know. I've told her that multitasking is **potentially / ironically** dangerous when you're driving.

Yarah   Well, **apparently / ideally** she didn't listen to either one of us.

Victoria   I guess not. But you know how some people are – they **ideally / inevitably** stick to their bad habits.

Yarah   True. Luckily she didn't get hurt. **Ideally / Evidently**, she'll learn her lesson from this. I mean, she can't possibly think it's OK to drive and talk on the phone after today!

B **Complete the conversation with the expressions in the box. Use one expression twice.**

can't possibly	couldn't possibly	evidently	ideally	ironically	potentially

A   Um, you know we have a test tomorrow, right? You _____[1] be studying and texting at the same time!

B   Oh, this is nothing! I could _____[2] watch TV, too, and still concentrate.

A   Seriously? If I were you, I _____[3] get anything done. _____[4], that's not a problem for you. I mean, you don't do your homework like this every day, do you?

B   Well, yeah. Multitasking just works for me, and _____[5] I seem to do even better when I do several things at once.

A   I guess it's possible. But according to an article I read, people _____[6] focus on more than one thing at a time. It also said that _____[7] you should work in a *totally* quiet room without any distractions.

About you

C **Complete the sentences with your own ideas.**

1. I can't possibly _____ and _____ at the same time.
2. Ideally, when I am studying, I _____ .
3. I think it is potentially dangerous to _____ .
4. Predictably, I get good grades when _____ .
5. I try to stay healthy by _____ . Supposedly, _____ is good for you.
6. I couldn't possibly _____ while I was watching TV.
7. Invariably, if I'm daydreaming in class, the teacher _____ .
8. Apparently, I'm in a better mood and easier to get along with when _____ .

Lesson D Reading E-books

A Prepare How do you think e-books have affected reading habits and book sales? Write three guesses. Then read the article to see if your ideas are mentioned.

Home   Local   World   **Technology**

E-books spur reading among Americans, survey shows

1   E-books aren't just becoming increasingly popular. They also appear to be promoting reading habits among American adults. So says new research from the Pew Internet and American Life Project, which states that about one-fifth of U.S. adults have read an e-book in the past year.

2   And if you expand that to include Americans over 16 who have used an e-reader device or app to read news articles or magazine-style features, the figure jumps to 43 percent.

3   E-book users tend to read more often than people who read only print material, Pew found. In particular, they read more books. A typical e-book user read 24 books in the past year, compared with the 15 books reported by typical non-e-book users.

4   Also, a third of people who read e-content say they now spend more time reading than they did before e-books. This is especially true for people who own tablets and e-book readers.

5   This might be good for the economy. According to Pew, e-book users are "also more likely than others to have bought their most recent book, rather than borrowed it, and they are more likely than others to say they prefer to purchase books in general."

6   E-readers and tablets (including Amazon's Kindle Fire e-reader, which is a modified Android tablet) were a popular holiday gift item last year. Currently 28 percent of Americans age 18 and older own at least one tablet or an e-book reader. And that's not even counting the people who read books on a smartphone or iPod Touch app.

7   Then again, Pew also noted that e-book users often start searching for books online — which isn't great news for people who run brick-and-mortar bookstores.

8   For now, print reading material still rules the consumer market, however. Pew found that nearly three-fourths of U.S. adults read a printed book in 2011, and 11 percent listened to an audio book. Print books are especially popular when people read to children.

9   Print books are also the most popular choice when people want to borrow or lend a book. That's not surprising — recently author Dave Taylor explained step-by-step how to borrow a Kindle book from a public library. It's not too difficult, but is still considerably more complicated than walking into the library and pulling a book off the shelf.

10   The survey also found that just slightly more people prefer e-books over print for reading in bed.

11   On the flip side, Pew noted that nearly 20 percent of U.S. adults said they had not read a single book in the past year. In general, people who don't own electronic reading devices are more likely not to read much at all.

12   In addition, nearly 20 percent of Americans 16 and older said they had "physical or health conditions that made reading difficult or challenging." Most of these people are older (25 percent of those over age 50), unemployed, or low-income. But an interesting aspect of e-book and audio book technology is its potential to improve the accessibility of written content.

13   Most e-reading devices allow the reader to adjust the font, font size, contrast, column width, and other factors to compensate for impaired vision. Plus, they often include text-to-speech technology that can read books or articles aloud — maybe not with thrilling delivery, but still a useful option. This can also be helpful to people with limited literacy.

14   The cost of e-reading devices keeps dropping, and it's likely that in the next year or two companies like Amazon may be giving away basic e-readers for free (on the principle that you can make more money selling "blades" than "razors").

15   As the price of e-readers approaches zero, it opens up more opportunities for people who have been left on the wrong side of the digital divide to access the same wealth of information, entertainment, and education as people with normal vision and average-or-better income.

16   Since the invention of writing, the written word has always disrupted the balance of power in societies. While e-books might have started out as a high-tech novelty for early adopters, they may ultimately prove to be a great equalizer across boundaries of ability, resources, and education.

SOURCE: www.cnn.com

B **Read for main ideas** **Read the article again. Check (✔) the true statements.**

☐ People who read e-books read more often than those who read print books.
☐ The majority of Americans under 18 own e-readers.
☐ The development of e-books has created economic problems for traditional bookstores.
☐ E-readers were still too expensive to be a popular gift for the holidays last year.
☐ People who read to children prefer print books to e-books.

C **Paraphrase** **Write the number of the paragraphs next to each description.**

1. The growing popularity of e-books may be affecting sales at bookstores. _____
2. The cost of e-readers means that more people with lower incomes can enjoy what e-books have to offer. _____
3. E-books may remove social, educational, and physical limitations, just as written word changed the balance of social powers. _____
4. E-book users are avid readers, more so than readers of print books. _____ , _____
5. Book sales have gone up because e-book users like to buy rather than borrow books. _____
6. E-books help those who have trouble reading due to certain disabilities. _____
7. Print books are more typically lent and borrowed. _____
8. E-readers have recently become a popular holiday gift. _____

D **Read for details** **Answer the questions. Check (✔) a, b, or c.**

1. According to the article, why are e-readers good for the economy?
   ☐ a. People buy more content to read.
   ☐ b. People go to more bookstores.
   ☐ c. People buy the e-book and the print book.
2. Why are print books more popular with people who go to the library?
   ☐ a. People find it easier to borrow a print book from the library.
   ☐ b. It's cheaper.
   ☐ c. both a and b
3. What is the principle that is driving companies to consider giving e-readers away?
   ☐ a. They can make more money by selling e-books than by selling the e-reading devices.
   ☐ b. They want readers with lower incomes to read more.
   ☐ c. They can ensure that customers will never buy print books again.
4. How are e-readers helping to bridge the digital divide?
   ☐ a. They are becoming so easy to operate that anyone can use one.
   ☐ b. They are attracting a wider audience because more e-books are being published.
   ☐ c. Their low cost means everyone can have access to information.

About you

E **React** **Answer the questions with your own opinions.**

1. What did you find most interesting about the article? Did anything surprise you?
   _____
   _____

2. Is the information in the article also true about people you know? In what way?
   _____
   _____

3. Do you prefer e-readers or print books? Why?
   _____
   _____

Writing   Describing graphs, charts, and tables

A   Look at the table. Then circle the best options to complete the article.

Internet access by age and location
2011 United States of America Census Data

Age	Total adults	At home	At work	At school or a library
18 to 34 years old	30.48	33.34	31.74	58.92
35 to 54 years old	37.77	41.31	50.09	29.93
55 years old and over	31.75	25.35	18.18	11.16

The table **shows / accounted for** where Americans accessed the Internet in 2010. As **accounted for / can be seen** in the table, 41.31 percent of 35 to 54 year olds used the Internet at home **as compared to / as shown** only 25.35 percent of those older than 55. **In comparison, / In contrast to** all other age groups, 58.92 percent of 18 to 34 year olds used the Internet at school or the library. Just over half of 35 to 54 year olds used the Internet at work, **accounted for / in comparison to** a third of 18 to 34 year olds and less than 20 percent of people 55 and over.

B   Complete the sentences about the table above using the expressions in the box. Use capital letters where necessary.

> accounted   as can be seen in   illustrates   in comparison with   in contrast   represented

1. The table _____ where people of different ages access the Internet.
2. _____ other age groups, those 55 years and older were less likely to go online at work.
3. However, the 55 years and over age group was least likely to use a library or school, which _____ for only 11.16 percent of that age group's place of Internet access.
4. The workplace _____ the most popular location for Internet access in the age group 35 to 54 years.
5. _____ the table, about a third of 18 to 34 year olds had Internet access at home.
6. _____ , just over a quarter of the older age group had Internet access at home.

C   Editing Correct the mistakes. There is one error in each sentence.

1. As it can be seen in the graph, the number of people using smartphones has increased.
2. In 2010, the number of Americans owning cell phones represented for 85 percent of the total population.
3. China has the highest number of Internet users, in comparison other countries.
4. According to the Pew Internet and American Life Project, e-book users read 24 books per year, compared print book readers, who only read 15 books per year.
5. In the past, a small group of "innovators," who accounted to two percent of consumers, were the first to buy hi-tech products.
6. As it is shown in the graph, the number of people who use the Internet on their phones has doubled.

D   Write a report on the table in Exercise A. Use expressions for describing and comparing information.

Listening extra The hazards of e-waste

A For each topic below, predict one fact that you would expect to hear about in a documentary about e-waste (old electronic equipment that is thrown away).

☐ cell phones and computers: <u>They end up in landfill sites.</u>
_____

☐ consumers who buy electronics: _____
_____

☐ oceans around the world: _____
_____

☐ possible health problems: _____
_____

☐ environmental problems: _____
_____

☐ animals and birds: _____
_____

☐ recycling: _____
_____

B 🔽 Listen to the documentary. Check the topics in Exercise A that are discussed.

C 🔽 Listen again. Are the sentences true or false? Write T or F.

1. Most consumers know what happens to their cell phones and laptops when they discard them. _____
2. All the possible health dangers from e-waste are known. _____
3. E-waste is often shipped to recycling centers in developing countries and taken apart. _____
4. Workers in recycling centers are always given protective clothing. _____
5. Exposure to lead can cause problems with the central nervous system. _____
6. The amount of e-waste produced is not expected to rise in the next few years. _____
7. Toxic chemicals from e-waste can get into groundwater supplies. _____
8. So far, regulation of e-waste has not been completely successful. _____

D 🔽 Listen to part of the documentary again. Answer the questions using the numbers in the box. There are two extra.

15–20%	50%	80–85%	20 million	30 million	50 million

1. How many tons of e-waste are produced every year? _____
2. How many computers does the U.S. throw away every year? _____
3. How much e-waste is reported as being recycled now? _____
4. How much e-waste goes to landfills each year? _____

About you

E Answer the questions with your opinions.

1. What do you think electronics companies can do to limit the amount of e-waste produced?
_____
_____

2. What do you think countries can or should do to deal with the issue of e-waste?
_____
_____

Now complete the *Unit 2 Progress chart* on page 98.

Unit 3 Society

Lesson A **Grammar** Linking events

A Complete the conversation with the participles in the box.

bearing	growing up	having worried	not being	speaking

Mark I don't understand why my friends need to replace their cell phones and tablets and stuff every year. I mean, _____[1] in sort of a poor family, I was taught never to spend money if I didn't absolutely have to.

Laura Yeah, but there's a lot of social pressure these days. I mean, _____[2] as someone who's bought four new cell phones in three years, I am obviously totally unable to resist the pressure.

Mark Well, _____[3] able to afford constant upgrades, I just try to be happy with what I have.

Laura But you could afford it if you decided it was a priority. I mean, _____[4] in mind how much people use technology, you have to keep up in some jobs.

Mark Yeah. I know. But _____[5] about it for some time, I've now decided I don't care if my stuff looks a little old fashioned. I'd rather spend my money on other things.

B Rewrite the article by replacing the underlined words with participle clauses. Delete unnecessary words and add punctuation if needed.

Do you feel pressured to buy the latest gadgets?

Natalie Sherman, SENIOR: "I come from a family that didn't have a lot of money, so I couldn't have all the things I wanted. As a teenager, I often felt embarrassed because I never had the same phone as my friends. I don't feel that way anymore."

Coming from a family that didn't have a lot of money, I couldn't have all the things I wanted.

_____
_____
_____
_____

Armando Lopez, FRESHMAN: "I grew up in a low-tech home, and I never felt the need to have all the latest technology. These days, I live in a university environment, so I feel much more pressure to keep up. And you know what? Because I don't want to look like I'm totally behind the times, yesterday I went out and spent a fortune on a new phone!"

_____
_____
_____
_____
_____
_____

Chung-hee Park, JUNIOR: "I'm a communications major, so I need to buy the latest phones, gadgets, apps, etc. I've thought about it, and I've stopped worrying about all the money I'm spending. I think of it as an education expense."

_____
_____
_____
_____
_____
_____

About you

C Answer the question from the article with your own information.

_____
_____

Lesson B Vocabulary New experiences

A Circle the best options to complete the *take* expressions in the post on a college website.

HOME   ABOUT   ACADEMICS   ADMISSIONS   COMMUNITY / CULTURE   ATHLETICS   **ASK QUESTIONS**   QUICK LINKS

I'm a freshman on a scholarship, and I'm so worried about my grades that I've been avoiding most social activities. It's making me a little depressed. Any suggestions? — LonelyFreshman asked - 27 minutes ago

I'm a sophomore now, but I know how you're feeling. In my freshman year, I wanted to do well, so I let my studies take **note of / precedence over** everything else. Whenever there were a lot of people around the dorm, I took **refuge / steps** in the library. My grades were pretty good, but I hadn't taken **into account / for granted** just how lonely I would feel. Finally, I took **precedence over / stock of** things and decided I needed to take **credit for / advantage of** some of the extracurricular activities here. Actually, it was my roommate who took **charge of / advantage of** the situation. He encouraged me to take **part in / stock of** some sports activities with him. And he can also take **credit for / note of** getting me involved in co-ed volleyball! Getting exercise and making friends makes me feel better, and my grades have actually gone up! — JB2020 - 10 minutes ago

B Complete the article with the *take* expressions in the box.

take advantage	take into account	take refuge	take steps	take time
take for granted	take note	take responsibility	take the initiative	

FIRST TRIP ABROAD?   Some dos and don'ts for the novice traveler

Before any trip, there are several _____ that you should _____ to prepare.

- Even if you're going on a guided tour, _____ for learning about the country before you go. Read about the country's history, cultural heritage, and social customs.
- Don't _____ that everyone you meet will understand English. Learn important phrases like "Hello," "Good-bye," "I'm sorry," and "Thank you" in the local language.

When you arrive, keep in mind the following things:

- Make sure you visit the most important museums and monuments, but also _____ each day to walk around the streets and spend an hour or so exploring the shops, markets, and local architecture.
- As you explore, _____ of the local customs so that you can behave or dress appropriately.
- If you feel people aren't being polite to you, remember to _____ that different cultures don't always follow the same rules. What seems rude in one country may actually be polite in another.
- If you know the local language, _____ to talk to servers and sales personnel in shops and stores. If you don't speak up first, they may address you in your own language and you'll lose the opportunity to practice.
- Be sure to get an early start each day, but don't be afraid to _____ in your hotel room when you feel really tired. You need to feel rested in order to _____ of all the wonderful things the culture has to offer.

About you

C Answer the questions with your own information. Use the underlined expressions.

1. Have you <u>taken part in</u> any new activities this year? _____

_____

2. What <u>takes precedence</u> in your life these days – your studies (or job) or your social activities?

_____

3. Have you ever <u>taken</u> something or someone <u>for granted</u> and then regretted it later?

_____

Lesson B Grammar Adding emphasis

A Circle the best options to complete the article on a website for young entrepreneurs.

As a young entrepreneur, I've had to face many challenges. The first was to convince people that I needed to drop out of college in order to start my own business. My parents were **such / so** upset that we barely spoke for months. **Even / Only** my best friend thought it was a bad idea. I finally realized that **only / even** I could make the decision, and so I went ahead with my plans. The second challenge was to find time for a social life. Building a business from the ground up was **such / so** hard work that I didn't **only / even** have the energy to go out for coffee with friends. A different sort of challenge came from the fact that I was **so / such** young, since some of my potential clients didn't think I was old enough to take on **such / only** a huge responsibility. I remember one of them saying, "You're **only / even** a college kid – how can you possibly be running a company?" Remarks like that were **such / so** discouraging that I wondered at times if I had made the wrong decision. Ultimately, though, I was just **such / so** committed to building a successful business that I refused to give up.

B Rewrite each pair of sentences as a single sentence, using *so . . . that* or *such . . . that*. Delete unnecessary words and add punctuation if needed.

1. Starting a new job is often a stressful experience. Even the most self-confident person can get nervous.

   Starting a new job is such a stressful experience that even the most self-confident
   person can get nervous.

2. Learning new skills can be a very demanding task. New employees often feel overwhelmed.

   _____

   _____

3. Employees are often embarrassed about not knowing something. As a result, they're afraid to ask for help.

   _____

   _____

4. Understanding a company's culture is a very important part of fitting in. Therefore, new employees need to make it a major priority.

   _____

   _____

5. Most employees eventually become very comfortable in their jobs. So they completely forget how hard things were in the beginning.

   _____

   _____

Lesson C Conversation strategies

A Complete the conversation with the words in the box.

again	but	having	so	then	though

Angela   I read this article yesterday where the author says women shouldn't wait too long before starting a family. She says they should have their children when they're in their early twenties.

Tamara   Wow. That's the opposite of what's happening in a lot of places. But then _____¹, maybe she has a point. It's easier to adapt to a big change in lifestyle when you're young.

Angela   That's true. But even _____², if a woman doesn't take a job right out of college, she may ruin her chances of having a career. _____³ said that, _____⁴, it's probably less risky for the baby.

Tamara   Yeah, I've heard that the older the parents are, the more likely it is there'll be problems.

Angela   Right, _____⁵ then there's the issue of maturity. That's why so many people don't get married until they're in their thirties.

Tamara   Yeah, and even _____⁶ some people don't seem mature enough to take on such a huge responsibility!

B Complete the conversation with contrasting views. Write the letters a–f.

a. life was very difficult for average people
b. I guess it's not that clear right now what's going to happen in the future
c. people's lives were just much simpler
d. in some ways I think opportunities are shrinking for lots of people
e. your grandfather probably didn't have as many opportunities as we have today
f. they don't have much job security

Roberto   I often think life used to be a lot less complicated years ago.

Sam   Well, yeah, but then again, _____¹. I mean, they had to work harder and had less free time.

Roberto   Maybe, but even so, _____² – not easier, but simpler. Probably because people had fewer choices to make. Take my grandfather, for example. After he graduated from college, he immediately got a good job, started a family, and stayed at the same company for 40 years.

Sam   OK, so that sounds like a stable life. But then again, _____³. In today's world, maybe he would have had a more exciting life.

Roberto   That's probably true. Even so, _____⁴. I mean, nowadays people have to work hard to land a good job. And even then, _____⁵. Companies are going out of business all the time.

Sam   Oh, that's just a temporary situation. You know, the economy is changing so fast with the Internet and all. But, having said that, _____⁶.

About you

C Complete the sentences with your own ideas.

1. They say it's better to start a family early in life. But then again, _____

_____

2. Life might be easier in some ways than it was in the past. Having said that, though, _____

_____

3. Young people today face more challenges than ever before. Even so, _____

_____

Lesson D Reading English and the Internet

A Prepare All of the following expressions owe their existence to the Internet. How many other examples can you think of?

an app	to blog	to friend someone	a pop-up ad	to scroll down

B Read the article. How many words from the article had you thought of in Exercise A?

THE CHANGING LANGUAGE OF THE INTERNET

1 Since its commercial explosion in the 1990s, the Internet has radically changed many aspects of our lives – the way we shop, how we communicate with each other, where we find out information, and, in some cases, where we work. It is even changing our very language, subtly but with great rapidity.

HOW THE INTERNET CHANGED THE ENGLISH LANGUAGE

2 Even the word "Internet" has changed since its inception. While once upon a time spelling out the word with anything other than a capital "I" at the front would earn you a sharp reproach for failing to address a proper noun with the respect it deserved, these days it is more acceptable to use a lowercase "i," denoting a common noun. Why? Possibly because the Internet was once a more definitive object in its own right, referring to a tangible network of computers, whereas today the Internet has become a more abstract concept referring to the jumbled multitudes of information that can be found online.

3 Similarly, a "web site" (as in, a site on the Web) formed a new compound noun long ago to become "website." This is just one example of the internet creating new language to describe the objects that exist within its virtual realms.

4 In many cases, the jury is still out on the specifics of these new terminologies that have been thrust into the English language, in many cases transitioning from buzzwords to everyday words within the click of a mouse.

5 "Electronic mail," once a wonderfully exotic signifier of a brave new age, has since become a word used casually dozens of times a day in offices and homes throughout the world. Since becoming a commonly used term, electronic mail has also become a compound noun, using only the first letter of the adjective part. But even some

dictionaries differ on the specifics, and forms of the word commonly seen include E-Mail, e-mail, E-mail, and email.

BLOGGERS BLOGGING ON THEIR BLOGS

6 "Blog" too has become a commonly used word in everyday conversation and serious journalism, to the extent that it's easy to forget it is a relatively recent blend, or portmanteau, of "web log." What's more, it's even given birth to its own verbs, i.e., "blogging" and "blog," and descriptive terms for people who indulge in such activities ("bloggers").

7 Google, meanwhile, is an impressive example of a proper noun that has become a verb synonymous with searching the Internet (to "google" something), within little more than a decade.

8 Even more recently, social networks have brought yet more neologisms to the table, and these days people are so busy "tweeting," "digging," and "friending," you'd be excused for mistaking the Internet for some sort of bizarre loved-up hippy commune.

9 Like it or not, the Internet is changing the way we use language at a tremendous pace. Once upon a time, new words would take decades or more to embed themselves in common use and dictionaries. Whereas today's instantaneous global communications mean the English language is very much at the mercy of whatever happens to be "trending" at the time.

SOURCE: www.writemysite.co.uk

C Read for main ideas **Choose the correct option to complete the sentences.**

1. The Internet is changing the English language _____ .
   a. in negative ways
   b. quickly
   c. extremely slowly
2. The author states that the word "internet" is often no longer capitalized because it now refers to _____ .
   a. a physical network of computers
   b. an abstract collection of online information
   c. a single, central computer
3. The word *blog* is an example of _____ .
   a. two words combined as one
   b. a foreign word
   c. an old word with a new meaning
4. An example of a name that people now use as a verb is _____ .
   a. blog
   b. google
   c. friend
5. Social networks have led to the creation of words such as _____ .
   a. *tweeting* and *friending*
   b. *hippy* and *loved-up*
   c. *googling* and *blogging*
6. Years ago, it took _____ for new words to appear in dictionaries.
   a. longer
   b. less time
   c. the same amount of time

D Guess words in context **Replace the words in bold with words and expressions from the article that have the same meanings.**

1. New words relating to the Internet are being added to the English language with great **speed**. (para. 1)
2. In the past, forgetting to use a capital letter might have received **harsh criticism**. (para. 2)
3. In many cases, **there is no definitive decision** on how to spell new Internet terms. (para. 4)
4. Many Internet terms began as **fashionable expressions** used by a select group of people. (para. 5)
5. The verb *google* now **means the same as** "search the Internet." (para. 7)
6. Dictionaries are rapidly adding many **newly created words** related to the Internet. (para. 7)
7. The English language is **extremely dependent on** the various websites and whatever is **being talked or written about** on the Internet. (para. 9)

About you

E React **Answer the questions with your own ideas and opinions.**

1. How has technology, such as cell phones and laptops, affected your writing?

   _____

   _____

2. Do you think linguists should be worried about new words entering the lexicon? Why or why not?

   _____

   _____

3. What new words have entered your language as a result of the Internet and social media?

   _____

   _____

Writing Writing an evaluation

A Circle the correct option to complete the evaluation.

The following is an evaluation of the Summer Intensive Program in Wildlife Conservation. In this report I will comment on the classroom instruction and the field trips, and I will conclude by offering a general recommendation.

The teachers in the program demanded a lot from the students. **Consequently, / Even so,** the students had to work extremely hard to meet their high standards. **In spite of / Because of** all the hard work required, we gained detailed knowledge of ecosystems and good conservation practices. The classes were lively with lots of teacher-student interaction, **giving / so** everyone the opportunity to participate. **Consequently / As a result of** the interactive teaching styles, all of the students got really involved in the classes.

The field trips, on the other hand, were not as well organized. Often the bus rides were **such / so** long that we did not have enough time to explore the habitats we were studying. In addition, some tour guides presented **so / such** detailed information that students felt overwhelmed. **Having said that, / As a result,** the field trips gave us a unique opportunity to observe wildlife that we had never seen before, **help / helping** us to understand more about conservation issues.

Generally speaking, the program was a success. Most students improved their knowledge of wildlife conservation. **Moreover, / Therefore,** I would recommend this program to anyone who would like a good background in this field in a short time.

B Rewrite these extracts from a report using the expressions in parentheses. Sometimes you need to rewrite two sentences as one.

1. Our summer course was incredibly useful. I strongly recommend that you sign up for it. (therefore)

   _____

2. The teachers always prepared their lessons carefully. We never wasted any class time. (as a result)

   _____

3. Sometimes the guides were in a hurry to finish their talks. It was hard to follow them. (such . . . that)

   _____

4. The wildlife cruise was led by a brilliant naturalist. It was very informative. (consequently)

   _____

5. Some of the lectures were too technical. They demotivated some students. (so . . . that)

   _____

C Editing Correct the mistakes. Sometimes there is more than one mistake and more than one correct answer. One sentence is correct.

1. The summer course was excellent therefore I'm planning to major in wildlife management.
2. The ocean mammals course was such difficult some students lost interest.
3. The classes finished late, give us no time to relax before the field trips.
4. I had never seen a whale before therefore I was excited to go on the wildlife cruise.
5. One problem was that we had no free days, leaving us all exhausted by the end of the week.
6. Our group project was so success so we got the highest grade in the class.

D Write an evaluation of your favorite teacher. Explain why you like him or her.

Listening extra Resisting social pressures

A **Match the words and definitions. Write the letters a–e.**

1. to pursue a goal _____
2. a convention _____
3. to defy _____
4. an obstacle _____
5. to conform _____

   a. to resist; to refuse to obey
   b. something that's in the way
   c. to obey; to follow rules
   d. to try to achieve an aim
   e. a rule or custom

B **Listen to an extract from a TV show. Are the sentences true or false? Write T or F.**

1. The talk show host thinks the topic of social pressure relates to everyone's life. _____
2. Susan has written several books about the psychology of social pressure. _____
3. Dr. Jones would like to settle into a more traditional life. _____
4. Jason was the first person in his family not to join the family business. _____
5. Susan thinks if people have a strong sense of personal identity, they can pursue their goals. _____
6. Jason was interested in a career in fashion, but still decided to become an artist. _____
7. Dr. Jones used to enjoy the same TV shows as other kids did. _____
8. Jason's family always understood that he wanted to choose art over business. _____

C **Listen again. Circle the correct option to complete each sentence.**

1. Susan **is / is not** the only person on the show who knows something about social pressure.
2. Dr. Jones works for **a hospital / several organizations**.
3. Dr. Jones is **single / married**.
4. As a child, Jason **did / did not** have a strong sense of his identity.
5. Growing up, Dr. Jones loved to watch **cartoons / documentaries** on TV.
6. Susan says that resisting social conventions is **difficult / natural**.

D **Answer the questions with your own ideas and opinions.**

About you

1. Why do you think most people conform to social norms?

   _____

   _____

2. Do you think that you are the kind of person who can resist social pressure? Why or why not?

   _____

   _____

3. Do you think that your society should allow people more freedom to make their own decisions about careers and family?

   _____

   _____

Now complete the *Unit 3 Progress chart* on page 98.

Amazing world

Lesson A Vocabulary Animal behavior

A **Match the words in bold with the words that have a similar meaning. Some sentences have two answers. Write the letters a–g.**

a. breed	b. burrows	c. colonies	d. feed	e. nest	f. predators	g. young

1. The European rabbit lives in **large groups** in Spain, Portugal, and parts of Africa. _____
2. These rabbits live in networks of **holes**, which are also known as warrens. _____
3. Typically, these rabbits **eat** at night to avoid being attacked by **animals that kill and eat others**. _____ , _____
4. European rabbits can begin to **reproduce** when they are just four months old. _____
5. During pregnancy, female rabbits make a **comfortable and safe home**, where they can give birth to their **babies**. _____ , _____

B **Complete the poster with the words in the box. Use each word only once.**

feed	hatch	hibernate	lay	mate	predators

— HELP SAVE THE MONARCH BUTTERFLIES! —

Did you know that millions of monarch butterflies die each year because of human activity? Did you know that the milkweed plant, which is essential to the butterflies' survival, is being destroyed at an alarming rate?

Interesting facts about monarch butterflies

Monarch butterflies fly south from North America before the winter begins. During the winter months, the butterflies _____[1] in Mexico, where the climate is mild. In February and March, the butterflies start to _____[2] in order to reproduce. The butterflies _____[3] their eggs on milkweed plants. When the larvae _____[4] , the caterpillars _____[5] on this same plant. In addition to providing food, the milkweed plant also gives the monarch butterflies poisonous chemicals that help them develop a defense against _____[6] , such as frogs, birds, mice, and lizards.

Join the discussion on our online forum and help save these remarkable creatures.

About you

C **Answer the questions with your own opinions.**

1. Write about an animal or insect. Say why you find it interesting.

   _____

   _____

2. What do you think is the most interesting aspect of insect, bird, and animal migration?

   _____

   _____

Lesson A Grammar Talking about the past in the future

A Circle the correct verb forms to complete the excerpt from a documentary. Sometimes both forms are possible.

Biologists have made many fascinating discoveries about black bear hibernation. For example, prior to hibernating later this year, this black bear **will have gained / will have been gaining** at least 30 pounds every week over a period of several months. By the time she is in hibernation next year, her heartbeat **will have dropped / will have been dropping** to just eight beats per minute from around 40 to 50. In addition, her body temperature **will have decreased / will have been decreasing** by 12 degrees Fahrenheit. By spring, she **will have hibernated / will have been hibernating** for six months, and **will have lost / will have been losing** about 30 percent of her body weight.

B Complete the sentences with the future perfect or future perfect continuous of the underlined verbs. Sometimes both forms are possible.

1. Around November, this pregnant polar bear will enter her nest, or den, to give birth and <u>rest</u>.
   In January, she ____will have been resting____ for two months.
2. These Siberian marmots <u>hibernate</u> for eight months – from October to May.
   By March, they _____ for five months.
3. A shark <u>loses</u> approximately 1,800 teeth per year.
   At the end of the year, it _____ approximately 1,800 teeth.
4. An anteater <u>eats</u> 210,000 ants per week.
   In two weeks, this anteater _____ 420,000 ants.
5. The average female vampire bat can <u>consume</u> 20 grams (1 fluid ounce) of blood in 20 minutes.
   After 10 minutes, she _____ 10 grams (.5 fluid ounces) of blood.
6. A blue whale calf <u>gains</u> about 90 kilograms (200 pounds) every 24 hours.
   In 48 hours, a blue whale calf _____ about 180 kilograms (400 pounds).

About you

C Answer the questions with your own views. Use the future perfect or future perfect continuous in your answers.

1. How do you think the natural world will have changed in 50 years?

   _____

   _____

   _____

   _____

2. Do you think that conservation efforts will have benefitted any species that are endangered in 50 years time?

   _____

   _____

   _____

   _____

Lesson B Grammar Combining ideas

A Use the prepositional expressions in the box to replace the underlined parts of the sentences. Write the letters a–f. Some have more than one correct answer.

a. apart from	c. in addition to	e. due to the fact
b. as a result of	d. in line with	f. thanks to

1. <u>Because of</u> their amazing survival skills, scorpions are able to live in some of the harshest environments. _____
2. <u>According to</u> biologists' criteria for the classification of snakes, there are approximately 13,000 venomous species. _____
3. <u>Besides</u> offering protection from predators, quills help porcupines stay camouflaged. _____
4. <u>As well as</u> being able to run up to 42 kilometers (26 miles) per hour, roadrunners can also fly. _____
5. Peregrine falcons have become an endangered species <u>because of</u> the effects of pesticides in their bodies and eggshells. _____
6. Since the 1800s, the prairie dog population has decreased <u>for the reason</u> that humans have destroyed their habitats to build towns and villages. _____

B Circle the best prepositional expressions to complete the information.

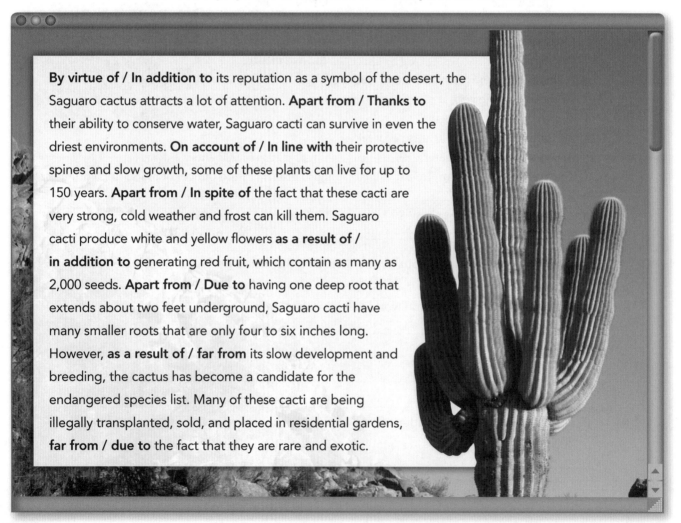

By virtue of / In addition to its reputation as a symbol of the desert, the Saguaro cactus attracts a lot of attention. **Apart from / Thanks to** their ability to conserve water, Saguaro cacti can survive in even the driest environments. **On account of / In line with** their protective spines and slow growth, some of these plants can live for up to 150 years. **Apart from / In spite of** the fact that these cacti are very strong, cold weather and frost can kill them. Saguaro cacti produce white and yellow flowers **as a result of / in addition to** generating red fruit, which contain as many as 2,000 seeds. **Apart from / Due to** having one deep root that extends about two feet underground, Saguaro cacti have many smaller roots that are only four to six inches long. However, **as a result of / far from** its slow development and breeding, the cactus has become a candidate for the endangered species list. Many of these cacti are being illegally transplanted, sold, and placed in residential gardens, **far from / due to** the fact that they are rare and exotic.

Lesson C Conversation strategies

A Complete the expressions using the words in the box.

also	event	in	mention	top

Prof. Taylor What do you think are the most urgent environmental problems?

Mario Well, global warming, but _____[1] it seems like water is another issue, especially since a third of the world's population doesn't have access to clean water.

Jennifer Yeah, I agree that water is major problem. On _____[2] of that, many of our fresh water sources are being polluted.

Fatima Not to _____[3] the amount of water used for agricultural purposes.

Will _____[4] any _____[5], we should manage water supplies better.

B Complete the conversation. Write the letters a–e.

> a. Not to mention the fact that fish is a major food source for billions of people.
> b. And also it's pretty bad that we allowed all that trash to collect in the first place.
> c. And what's more, they've even found hazardous waste.
> d. In any event, it's really bad for marine life.
> e. And on top of that, dolphins die because they get tangled up in trash.

Anthony Did you watch that show about the Great Pacific Garbage Patch?

Sara Yeah, I did. It was really disturbing.

Felipe I didn't see it. What is it?

Anthony Well, there's this huge trash dump floating in the middle of the Pacific. _____[1] I mean, can you imagine? Hazardous waste in the ocean?

Felipe So does that toxic stuff end up in the fish we eat?

Sara I guess. _____[2] You know, they drown.

Anthony Yeah. _____[3]

Sara Well, they'll have to do something about it to keep the oceans clean. _____[4]

Felipe Yeah, people depend on it. So, is anyone doing anything to clean it all up?

Sara Unfortunately not. It's seems like it's a complicated problem.

Anthony Well, if you ask me, it's appalling. _____[5]

C Circle the best expressions to complete the conversation.

A I was just reading this article about how the Siberian tiger is on the endangered species list.

B Really? I didn't think that tigers had any predators.

A Well, they don't – except humans. The biggest problems that affect them are pollution and deforestation. But **in any case, / and then** there *are* a lot of people who hunt them.

B Huh. I guess people still enjoy the challenge of hunting them. **In addition, / Not to mention** the fact that their fur is pretty valuable.

A Yeah. **And then / In any event**, they're hunted for body parts, too. **Also / In any case**, I think we should join an environmental group. Maybe we can do something.

Lesson D Reading Animals and earthquakes

A **Prepare** **How do you think some animals detect an earthquake? What unusual behaviors do they display before an earthquake? Check (✔) the boxes.**

Detection
- ☐ They feel the temperature drop.
- ☐ They detect the earth moving.
- ☐ They notice changes in chemistry.

Behavior
- ☐ They remain in water.
- ☐ They leave their mating sites.
- ☐ They become magnetic.

B **Read the article. Check your guesses from Exercise A.**

Toads able to detect earthquake days beforehand, study says

1 Toads may be able to detect earthquakes days before they hit, according to a study which reveals how the creatures deserted their mating site before Italy's L'Aquila quake last year. Toads may be able to detect imminent earthquakes, according to scientists. The finding will add to the accounts through the centuries where animals, from dogs to rats, snakes, and chickens, are said to have behaved strangely before an earthquake.

2 In the study published today in the *Journal of Zoology*, a colony of toads deserted their mating site three days before an earthquake struck in L'Aquila — the epicenter was 74 kilometers from the area where the animals had normally gathered. No toads returned to the site until 10 days later, after the last of the significant aftershocks had finished.

3 The discovery was made by accident by Rachel Grant, a life scientist at the Open University. She was studying the effects of lunar cycles on the toads' behavior and reproduction. "I was going out every evening at dusk and counting how many toads were active and how many pairs there were. Normally they arrive for breeding in early March and you get large numbers of males at the breeding site. The females get paired fairly quickly. They stay active and obvious around the breeding site until the spawning is over in April or May."

4 One day she noticed there were no toads. "Sometimes during the breeding season you get a drop in numbers if there's been a very cold night, but usually the day after, they come back again. It was very unusual that there was none at all."

5 There could be several mechanisms for animals to sense the beginnings of an earthquake, wrote Grant in the *Journal of Zoology*. They could detect seismic waves directly or ground tilt (which can occur in the minutes before a quake). In addition, there might be anomalies in the earth's magnetic field.

6 Looking for clues to explain the toads' behavior, Grant found that scientists had noticed disruptions in the ionosphere, the uppermost electromagnetic layer of the earth's atmosphere, at the time of the L'Aquila earthquake, which the toads may have detected. Previous earthquakes have had similar ionospheric disruptions associated with them. "I've spoken to seismologists who said there were a lot of gases released before the earthquake, a lot of charged particles. Toads and amphibians are very sensitive to changes in environmental chemistry, and I think these gases and charged particles could have been detected by the toads."

7 Previously, fish, rodents, and snakes have been anecdotally associated with unusual behavior more than a week before an earthquake or at distances greater than 50 kilometers.

8 In 2003, Japanese doctor Kiyoshi Shimamura said that there was a jump in dog bites and other dog-related complaints before and after earthquakes. Before the 1995 earthquake in Kobe, a disaster that killed more than 6,000 people, he found that accounts of dogs barking "excessively" went up by 18 percent on average in the months before the earthquake. Above the epicenter on Awaji Island, there was a 60 percent increase in complaints compared with a year earlier.

9 Grant's work is not the first time toads have been associated with sensing the precursors of earthquakes. "In 2008, there was a big earthquake in Szechuan province in China, and there was unusual migration of toads seen," she said. "I'd like to study it further and look at animal behavior in combination with seismological and geophysical precursors."

SOURCE: *The Guardian*

C Paraphrase Find the paragraph that each the sentence summarizes.

1. Toads might have felt the variations in gases in the earth's atmosphere. _____
2. There have been many stories about the changes in fish, snake, and rodent behavior before an earthquake or natural disaster. _____
3. Recent research shows that toads might be able to predict earthquakes. _____
4. Grant noticed the toads' change in behavior while conducting an unrelated study. _____
5. Others have noticed the change in toads' behavior before an earthquake. _____
6. Toads left their mating site before the L'Aquila earthquake. _____

D Check your understanding Answer the questions. Check (✔) a, b, or c.

1. How did scientists discover that toads might be able to detect earthquakes?
   a. They started hibernating early.
   b. They left the places where they normally breed.
   c. They stopped breeding for several months.

2. What was Rachel Grant studying when she made her discovery?
   a. the migration pattern of toads
   b. the impact of earthquakes on the toads' behavior
   c. the effect of the moon on the toads' mating behavior

3. What does Grant think affected the toads before the earthquake?
   a. a change in temperature
   b. a change in the weather patterns
   c. a change in the environmental chemistry

4. What was one of Kiyoshi Shimamura's discoveries about the Kobe earthquake?
   a. Reports of dog barking increased by 18 percent.
   b. Toads left their mating site.
   c. The number of dog bites decreased by 60 percent.

E Read for detail Are the sentences true or false, or is the information not given in the article? Write T, F, or NG. Correct the false sentences.

1. Two days before an earthquake struck in L'Aquila, toads left their mating sites. _____
2. Toads are nocturnal and mate at night. _____
3. Animals might be able to feel seismic waves. _____
4. Grant thinks that toads can sense a change in the gases released before an earthquake. _____
5. Before every earthquake in Japan, dog barking has increased. _____
6. In the 2008 earthquake in China, toads followed their usual migration patterns. _____

About you

F React Answer the questions with your own opinions.

1. What was the most interesting aspect of the article?

_____

_____

2. What did you learn from the article?

_____

_____

Writing A persuasive essay

A Read the introduction to a persuasive essay. What is the author's argument? What evidence does the author present as support? Then circle the correct prepositions.

Can animals predict natural disasters?

The belief that animals can predict earthquakes has existed for centuries **throughout / in terms of** Asia, but was largely based **beneath / upon** anecdotal evidence. Until fairly recently, the idea was dismissed **within / upon** the scientific community. However, research has shown that some species may well be able to sense changes in the earth's environment **amongst / within** a short time of a natural disaster occurring. Studies have revealed that **prior to / beneath** an earthquake, toads alter their breeding and migration habits, and dogs tend to bark more. Likewise, fish exhibit signs of panic when exposed to electromagnetic pulses similar to those of an earthquake. Taken together, the behavioral changes of toads, fish, and dogs appear to confirm the belief **amongst / in terms of** many ancient cultures that animals are sensitive to environmental changes caused by natural disasters and therefore can be said to predict them.

B Complete the paragraph with the expressions in the box.

amongst	beneath	in terms of	throughout	upon	within

Studying the behavior of animals can save lives. _____¹ history, people have depended _____² animals to predict natural disasters. One example is the 1975 earthquake in Haicheng, China. Biologists guessed that snakes and earthworms must have detected electromagnetic changes _____³ the earth's surface because they suddenly left their warm burrows in the middle of winter. The biologists then alerted the authorities of a possible earthquake, and _____⁴ 24 hours the city was evacuated. After the magnitude 7.3 earthquake struck, officials realized that with all the destruction, many people might have been killed. _____⁵ scientists, the credibility of this story has been debated. However, one can clearly see that _____⁶ saving lives, such a prediction was highly valuable for the residents of Haicheng.

C Editing **Correct the mistakes in these sentences. One sentence is correct.**

1. Many scientists disagree the idea that animals can predict earthquakes.
2. Scientists are now looking upon changes in animal behavior before natural disasters in greater detail.
3. Scientists cannot rely anecdotal evidence to prove their point.
4. If you look upon the facts, it seems certain that the climate is changing.
5. In the future, humans might depend our pets to predict natural disasters.
6. Some scientists look upon ancient beliefs about animals as superstition.

D Write a persuasive essay to answer the question: *Are animals smarter than humans think?* State your opinion and support your ideas with evidence.

Listening extra Remarkable raccoons

A Look at the photos. What do you know about raccoons? Check (✔) the adjectives you would use to describe these raccoons.

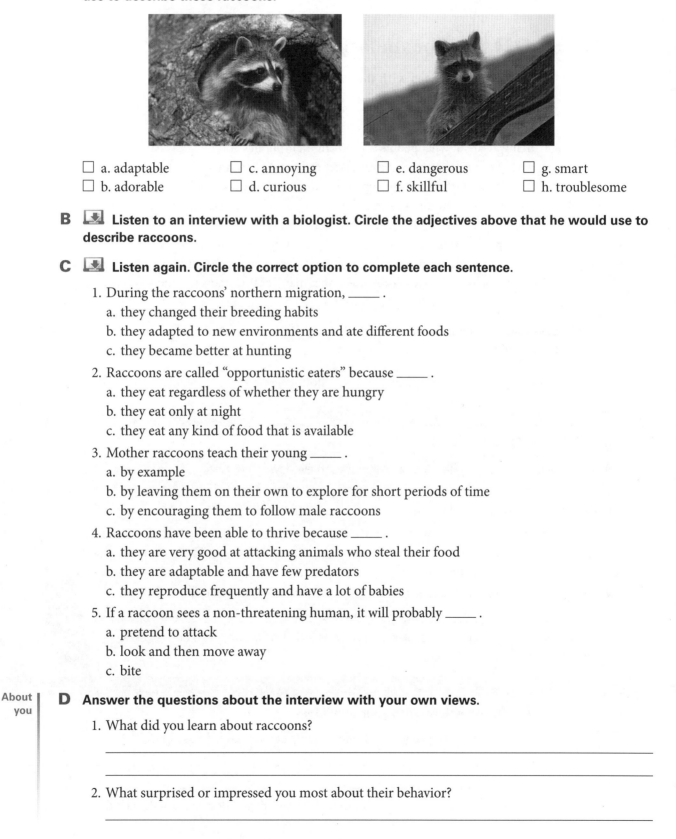

☐ a. adaptable ☐ c. annoying ☐ e. dangerous ☐ g. smart
☐ b. adorable ☐ d. curious ☐ f. skillful ☐ h. troublesome

B Listen to an interview with a biologist. Circle the adjectives above that he would use to describe raccoons.

C Listen again. Circle the correct option to complete each sentence.

1. During the raccoons' northern migration, _____ .
   a. they changed their breeding habits
   b. they adapted to new environments and ate different foods
   c. they became better at hunting

2. Raccoons are called "opportunistic eaters" because _____ .
   a. they eat regardless of whether they are hungry
   b. they eat only at night
   c. they eat any kind of food that is available

3. Mother raccoons teach their young _____ .
   a. by example
   b. by leaving them on their own to explore for short periods of time
   c. by encouraging them to follow male raccoons

4. Raccoons have been able to thrive because _____ .
   a. they are very good at attacking animals who steal their food
   b. they are adaptable and have few predators
   c. they reproduce frequently and have a lot of babies

5. If a raccoon sees a non-threatening human, it will probably _____ .
   a. pretend to attack
   b. look and then move away
   c. bite

About you

D Answer the questions about the interview with your own views.

1. What did you learn about raccoons?

_____

_____

2. What surprised or impressed you most about their behavior?

_____

_____

Now complete the *Unit 4 Progress chart* on page 99. Unit 4: Amazing world **33**

Lesson A Vocabulary Gadgets

A Complete the sentences with the words in the box.

compact	functional	innovative	integral	obsolete	portable

1. Being aware of what people want from their phones and devices is a/an _____ part of our marketing strategy. It's central to what we do.
2. It is also important to come up with our own new ideas and be _____ .
3. Of course our products need to be _____ and do what people want them to do, but attractive design is also important nowadays.
4. Most people want devices that are easy to carry – in other words, _____ .
5. They also want phones that are _____ enough to fit into a purse or pocket.
6. As technology changes faster and faster, many of this year's products will become _____ in two years' time.

B Complete the article with the words in the box. Sometimes more than one answer is possible.

countless	humble	rudimentary	significant	standard

A short history of cell phones

It seems difficult to imagine life without cell phones these days. Over time, they have become a _____[1] accessory, which most of us never leave home without. They have affected our ability to communicate and interact with the world in _____[2] ways.

The development of the technology in the U.S. started in the 1940s, and the first mobile phone call was made from an automobile in 1946. Martin Cooper, who worked for Motorola, is credited with making the first call from a handheld phone in 1973. The design of that phone seems _____[3] now. It weighed 1.13 kilos (2.5 pounds) and was 22.8 centimeters (9 inches) long!

Since those _____[4] beginnings, there have been _____[5] developments in both technology and design. The result is that phones today are viewed as a convenience that most of us would not want to live without.

About you

C Answer the questions with your own ideas.

1. What was the last gadget you bought? How has it changed your life?

_____

_____

2. What do you feel is the most innovative or significant device from the last decade? Why?

_____

_____

Lesson A Grammar Information focus 1

A Read the article. Write the adverb in parentheses in the correct place. Sometimes more than one answer is possible.

Who wouldn't want a personal jetpack? Ever since James Bond was seen launching off in the 1965 movie *Thunderball,* the personal jetpack has ___ —___ been ___eagerly___¹ anticipated (eagerly) as an alternative form of transportation. We are still waiting. However, innovative gadgets are _____ being _____² invented (continually) in the fields of transportation, energy, and communication – at even faster rates than ever before.

The amount of money that has _____ been _____³ injected (reportedly) into the development of new technology in the last decade is unprecedented. Every major corporation – and every new company – wants to be the first to come out with the next bestselling idea. With the kind of money that is _____ being _____⁴ invested (heavily) in these fields, there will definitely be more ground-breaking innovation – even if we do not know what it is yet. This is especially true because most of the research and development of new technologies has _____ been _____⁵ done (apparently) under a shield of secrecy.

And, what about that personal jetpack? I would bet that development is _____ being _____⁶ worked on (still) somewhere. I plan to be one of the first in line when it finally comes onto the market!

B Rewrite the sentences. Rewrite the underlined clauses in the passive and add the adverbs given. Sometimes there is more than one correct word order.

1. They were developing hybrid cars (intensively) long before they were on the market.
   _____

2. In fact, they have made hybrid cars (apparently) since the beginning of the auto industry.
   _____

3. Someone had built a hybrid car (already) in 1899.
   _____

4. They had presented that hybrid car (originally) at the 1900 World Fair in Paris.
   _____

5. It was a long time before they were mass producing hybrid cars (finally) in the 1990s.
   _____

6. It seems incredible, but by the end of 1997 they had sold only 300 hybrid cars. (reportedly)
   _____

7. Today, they are improving the designs, (continually) and people are driving hybrid cars.
   (increasingly) _____

About you

C Answer the questions with your own ideas.

1. What changes do you imagine are currently being worked on for the next generation of cars?
   _____

2. Which of the gadgets that you use have been significantly improved over recent years?
   _____

Lesson B Grammar Information focus 2

A Rewrite the underlined parts of the article using the passive forms of past modal verbs.

In May 2010, Jessica Watson completed a round-the-world solo voyage, arriving in Sydney Harbour just three days before her seventeenth birthday. Her journey was not without danger or controversy.

Certainly, Jessica sailed through some dangerous waters and, indeed, <u>something could easily have killed her.</u> _she could easily have been killed._ [1] The list of risks was long. <u>Pirates could have attacked her.</u> _____ [2] <u>Larger vessels could have also hit her sailboat</u> _____ [3] – indeed such an incident occurred prior to her voyage. Bad weather was a constant danger and <u>heavy seas might well have damaged or destroyed her boat.</u> _____ [4] And, in a worst case scenario, she could have fallen overboard and <u>sharks might have attacked her.</u> _____ [5]

Despite the risks, Jessica survived, but there was a lot of controversy around her trip because of her age. Many people felt that <u>her parents should not have allowed such a young person</u> _____ [6] to undertake a dangerous trip. People say <u>they ought not to have permitted it</u> _____. [7]

B Rewrite the sentences in the passive.

1. They should have made her parents stop her.
   Her parents should have been made to stop her.

2. They might have made her call the authorities every day.
   _____

3. They shouldn't have made her parents feel guilty.
   _____

4. They could have made her go with an older person.
   _____

5. They should have made her gain more experience before her first solo trip.
   _____

6. They could have made her wait until she was older to take the trip.
   _____

About you

C Answer the questions with your own ideas and opinions.

1. Think of a recent achievement by someone in the news. What are some things that might have happened to bring about a different result?
   _____
   _____

2. What was one thing that you were made to do when you were a child that you now realize helped you to become who you are today?
   _____
   _____

Lesson C Conversation strategies

A **Circle the correct expressions to complete the conversation.**

Clara I think it's always fascinating to read about the research that's going on. I mean, **just think about it / to put it another way**. It just seems like everything scientists do leads to some breakthrough.

Emma Well, **definitely / not necessarily**. I mean, **look at it this way: / let me put it another way:** they've spent billions trying to cure the common cold. I mean, yes, you can take medicine, but it doesn't cure your cold or stop you from getting one. **To put it another way, / Just think,** research doesn't always lead to something useful.

Clara **Maybe not / Just think**. But it's still worth doing. I mean, **just think about it / one way to look at it is** that you don't really know if you're going to make progress until you actually do the research. That's just the way it is.

Emma Yeah. I guess there is no way to know.

B **Match the sentences and responses. Write the letters a–e. There is one extra response.**

1. Do you think world peace is possible? _____
2. Don't you think a lot of money has been completely wasted on unnecessary medical research in recent years? _____
3. I think more research effort should be put into studying the oceans. We could learn a lot from that. _____
4. It seems like so much money has been put into space exploration and most of it's been wasted. _____

a. Absolutely. They haven't really been fully explored and you never know what might be discovered there.
b. Maybe, but there's already been a lot of research on animals.
c. Probably not. There'll always be something people are fighting about.
d. Not necessarily. There have been countless discoveries that have come from it, either directly or indirectly. Think of satellite technology, for example. I think it's been valuable.
e. Definitely not. I think any research is worth it. You never know what treatments or cures might be discovered.

C **Complete the conversation with the expressions in the box. Some may have more than one correct answer.**

Absolutely	Let me put it another way	Look at it this way	Maybe	✓ Not necessarily

Stephan I think scientists spend more and more money on research that seems so useless.

Andrea <u>Not necessarily</u> [1]. It may seem useless, but you never know what they might discover. _____ [2]. There are quite a few scientific discoveries that happened purely by chance. For example, those sticky notes that we all use . . . they're really convenient, aren't they?

Stephan _____ [3]. I use them all the time.

Andrea Well, the inventor was trying to make a strong glue, and he thought he'd failed. But, it turns out that he'd created something useful. So it wasn't a waste of time.

Stephan _____ [4]. I don't know. . . . That's not saving lives though, is it?

Andrea _____ [5]. Penicillin saves lives, and that was discovered by accident.

Lesson D   Reading   Pen and paper

A   Prepare What did people write on before the invention of paper? Make a list. Then scan the article to see how many of your ideas are included.

B   Read for topic Read the article. What was the main challenge in the development of a writing surface?

   a. making it inexpensive
   b. developing something easy to make and carry
   c. finding a writing instrument to use on the surface

THE INVENTION OF PAPER

1   Written communication has been the center of civilization for centuries. Most of our important records are on paper. Although writing has been around for a long time, paper hasn't.

2   In fact, putting thoughts down in written form wasn't always easy or practical. Early people discovered that they could make simple drawings on the walls of caves, which was a great place for recording thoughts, but wasn't portable.

3   Imagine spending hours scratching a message into a heavy clay tablet and then having to transport it. That's exactly what the Sumerians did around 4000 BCE. Although this form of written communication was now portable, it still wasn't practical because of its weight.

4   For centuries, people tried to discover better surfaces on which to record their thoughts. Almost everything imaginable was tried. Wood, stone, ceramics, cloth, bark, metal, silk, bamboo, and tree leaves were all used as a writing surface at one time or another.

5   The word *paper* is derived from the word *papyrus,* which was a plant found in Egypt along the lower Nile River. About 5,000 years ago, Egyptians created "sheets" of papyrus by harvesting, peeling, and slicing the plant into strips. The strips were then layered, pounded together, and smoothed to make a flat, uniform sheet.

6   No major changes in writing materials were to come for about 3,000 years. The person credited with inventing paper is a Chinese man named Ts'ai Lun. He took the inner bark of a mulberry tree and bamboo fibers, mixed them with water, and pounded them with a wooden tool. He then poured this mixture onto a flat piece of coarsely woven cloth and let the water drain through, leaving only the fibers on the cloth. Once dry, Ts'ai Lun discovered that he had created a quality writing surface that was relatively easy to make and was lightweight. This knowledge of papermaking was used in China before word was passed along to Korea, Samarkand, Baghdad, and Damascus.

7   By the tenth century, Arabians were substituting linen fibers for wood and bamboo, creating a finer sheet of paper. Although paper was of fairly high quality now, the only way to reproduce written work was by hand, a painstaking process.

8   By the twelfth century, papermaking reached Europe. In 1448, Johannes Gutenberg, a German, was credited with inventing the printing press. (It is believed that moveable type was actually invented hundreds of years earlier in Asia.) Books and other important documents could now be reproduced quickly. This method of printing in large quantities led to a rapid increase in the demand for paper.

SOURCE: Wisconsin Paper Council

C Information flow Put the following important events in the development of paper into chronological order.

_____ a. Papermaking occurred in China.
_____ b. Arabians substituted linen fibers for wood.
_____ c. Clay tablets are used by the Sumerians.
_____ d. The printing press is invented in Germany.
_____ e. Egyptians created sheets of papyrus.
_____ f. People discovered cave walls were a good place for drawings.

D Read for detail Are the sentences true or false, or is the information not given in the article? Write T, F, or NG. Correct the false sentences.

1. Cave paintings drawn by early people have been found all over the world. _____
2. Sumerians used clay tablets for writing around 3000 BCE. _____
3. At one time, tree leaves and tree bark were tried as a surface for writing. _____
4. Papyrus is found near water in Egypt. _____
5. There are three steps in the process of making paper from papyrus. _____
6. Egyptians used plants to make a kind of ink for writing on papyrus. _____
7. An Egyptian man is credited with inventing the first real paper. _____
8. Ts'ai Lun used plant fibers only in the process of making paper. _____
9. Ts'ai Lun worked on his process for making paper for many years before he was successful. _____
10. People were making paper in Korea, Samarkand, Baghdad, and Damascus at the same time as Ts'ai Lun in China. _____
11. The paper made by Arabians was better quality than previous paper. _____
12. Johannes Gutenberg invented moveable type and the printing press. _____
13. The invention of the printing press led to an increase in demand for paper. _____
14. Important documents are frequently kept in a digital or 'paperless' format. _____

About you

E React Answer the questions with your own ideas and opinions.

1. Which stage in the development of paper do you think was most important? Why?

_____

_____

2. How do you think the invention of the printing press changed the course of human development and history?

_____

_____

3. What do you think is the future of paper? Do you think paper will become obsolete?

_____

_____

Writing An opinion essay

A Read the introduction to an opinion essay. Which statement would the writer agree with — a, b, or c?

    a. Schools should only teach keyboarding skills.
    b. Schools should only teach handwriting.
    c. Schools should teach both keyboarding and handwriting.

Writing by hand vs. writing digitally: Same or different?

    It has been suggested that the art of writing with a pen or pencil is not worth teaching anymore. It is generally recognized that young people are already more comfortable working on a computer or tablet screen than on paper. Certainly, the skill of good handwriting is no longer as respected as it used to be. It often seems the only reason to learn how to write in cursive these days is to write signatures. However, there are those who disagree that there is no value in teaching handwriting anymore. For example, some say that writing digitally does not involve the same thought process as writing with a pen or pencil. They question whether writing digitally affects creativity differently than handwriting. I agree that writing digitally and writing by hand are likely very different processes. However, I would argue that completely replacing handwriting with keyboarding could lead to a loss, whether a loss in creativity or a loss that we have not even realized yet.

B Rewrite the sentences using *it* clauses in the passive.

    1. People generally accept that there will be less need for paper in the future.
       It is generally accepted that there will be less need for paper in the future.

    2. People widely recognize that fewer people are printing documents because they can store them electronically.

    3. People often suggest that there are many aspects of our current lives that will not be preserved for the future because of the absence of paper documents, such as personal letters.

    4. People have also suggested that the reading process on a screen may differ from the process of reading a printed book.

    5. People generally recognize that digital storage is an environmentally friendly option.

C Editing Correct the mistakes. There is one error in each sentence.

    1. Do you believe that writing on a screen, rather than paper, effects creativity in any way?
    2. Nevertheless writing on a computer might be faster than writing by hand, many wonder whether writing skills are being lost in the process.
    3. Researchers are not yet sure whether the affects of new technology are positive or negative for students.
    4. In the one hand, writing on a computer or tablet is faster. On the one hand, it doesn't work if there is a power outage and your battery runs out.

D Write an opinion essay to answer the question: *Should elementary schools stop teaching students how to write in cursive and use the time for other subjects?* Support your opinion with reasons and examples.

Listening extra New apps

A Look at the photo. Which of these apps are you familiar with? What other apps do you use? How often do you use them? Complete the chart.

Use multiple times a day:	
Use once or twice a day:	
Use a few times a week:	
Use occasionally:	
Never use:	

B Listen to the conversation. Circle the correct option to complete each sentence.

1. Pieter shows Aisha a music app that
   a. they both want.   b. they both have.   c. Aisha doesn't know about.

2. Pieter mentions
   a. one idea for an app.   b. two ideas for apps.   c. no ideas for apps.

3. Aisha mentions
   a. one idea for an app.   b. two ideas for apps.   c. no ideas for apps.

4. Their app ideas are
   a. all practical and functional.   b. all for amusement and fun.   c. both practical and fun.

C Listen again. Are the sentences true or false? Write T or F.

1. Pieter's app would only be helpful to find ATMs. _____
2. The name of Pieter's app is "Where's the nearest . . . ?" _____
3. Aisha thinks Pieter's app idea is original and new. _____
4. Aisha has two ideas for apps, and both are very amusing ideas. _____
5. One of Aisha's apps would help people keep track of money they save. _____
6. Pieter thinks ease of use would be important for this app. _____
7. Aisha's other app would use cartoon characters. _____
8. Aisha knows which cartoon character she would like to be. _____

About you

D Answer the questions.

1. Do you use any of the apps mentioned? Would you like to? Why or why not?

_____

2. What new app would you like to see? What would it do?

Now complete the *Unit 5 Progress chart* on page 99.

Business studies

Lesson A Grammar Adding and modifying information

A Read the article on advertising. Complete the relative clauses.

ADVERTISING: Can it become counterproductive?

Research shows that the popularity of a product depends greatly on the amount and extent of advertising. Repeated exposure to ads can produce positive feelings in potential customers, some __of whom__ [1] will become consumers of the product.

Moreover, successful advertising campaigns, some _____ [2] continue for 10 years or more, can ensure that a brand name will become firmly fixed in people's minds. Research also shows, however, that there is a tipping point at _____ [3] an ad campaign can become counterproductive. This happens when the customers to _____ [4] the product is targeted become overexposed, causing their positive feelings to become negative. It's not clear, however, how this research applies to Internet pop-up ads, most _____ [5] are universally disliked, as they often cover up material people are trying to read. Pop-up ads would appear to be counterproductive, as they rarely produce positive feelings in Internet users, almost all _____ [6] find them extremely intrusive. Nevertheless, some research shows that pop-up ads are actually very successful, and the prediction is that people will soon find them just as acceptable as other forms of advertising.

B Read the comments posted by readers of the article. Rewrite each first sentence using a relative clause with a pronoun or a preposition after the underlined word.

Laidback: Pop-up ads are an interesting <u>topic</u>, and I'm only too familiar with this topic, unfortunately. They're so annoying.
1. _Pop-up ads are an interesting topic, with which I'm only too familiar, unfortunately._

MadBrad: Every day I struggle with <u>pop-up ads</u>, and some of them can't be closed with a simple click. A click just takes you to their website!
2. _____

CoolHead: I don't pay much attention to <u>pop-up ads</u> as most of them advertise products I'm not interested in anyway. I ignore them.
3. _____

Maggie95: Absolutely – I can tell you that none of my <u>friends</u> can stand pop-up ads and most of them spend long hours on the Internet.
4. _____

Dino: Well, this is an interesting <u>phenomenon</u>, and a lot has been written about it. Negative feelings are often directed at the website, not the product.
5. _____

PennyPincher: Well, I subscribe to an Internet <u>service</u>, and I pay a lot of money for it every month. So why do I have to look at ads just to get into my email?
6. _____

BroadView: This is a difficult <u>problem</u>, and there seems to be no obvious solution to it. Advertising is here to stay.
7. _____

Kittie: Yes, websites are offering us a valuable <u>service</u>, and they have to pay for it with advertising. It's no different from television.
8. _____

Lesson B Vocabulary Attracting and deterring

A Read the list of dos and don'ts for people studying to get their realtors' license. Circle the best option to complete each piece of advice.

1. If you are trying to **woo / intimidate** new clients, listen to them carefully and refer often to what they have said in order to show you understand their needs and concerns.
2. Keep your car clean! Driving clients around in a messy or dirty car tends to **persuade them / put them off**, making it likely they will look for another realtor.
3. Don't show clients homes that are above their price range at the beginning. This can **scare them off / tempt them**. Instead, start out by showing them a property in their price range that won't **coax / appeal** to them.
4. Never **discourage / entice** clients by telling them a property is too expensive for them.
5. Never try to **pressure clients into / deter clients from** buying a property they don't really want because they won't be happy, and they won't recommend you to their friends.
6. The best way to **alienate / attract** new clients is through word of mouth. So treat all clients with care and respect so they will recommend you to their friends.

B Complete the conversation about renting an apartment with the correct forms of the verbs in the box. Sometimes there is more than one correct answer.

attract	convince	discourage	draw . . . in	lure	pressure . . . into	put . . . off

A I hear you're looking for an apartment.

B Yeah, well, I was hoping to live with my parents a bit longer, but they _____[1] me that it was time to find my own place, you know, now that I have a job.

A Have you seen any good possibilities?

B Not really. Actually, I'm not happy with my realtor. She's always trying to _____ me _____[2] renting places that I don't like. I get the feeling she doesn't listen to anything I say.

A I don't know why some realtors act like that. How do they expect to _____[3] new clients if they treat people that way? So how did you find this company?

B Well, they _____[4] me with this ad for a luxury apartment with low rent. But even though I called them immediately, the apartment was no longer available! They had other places to show me, but of course they were all more expensive.

A Oh, I know. It's a case of deceptive advertising. They do that to _____ new customers _____[5].

B Yeah, that's something that really _____ me _____[6]. But I've heard that all management companies do it.

A Well, don't let that _____[7] you. I'm sure you'll find something suitable.

About you

C Answer the questions with vocabulary from Exercises A and B where possible.

1. Have you ever been lured by a deceptive ad? What happened exactly?

   _____

   _____

2. Has a salesperson ever tried to pressure you into buying something? How did you feel about it?

   _____

   _____

Lesson B Grammar Referring to people and things

A Circle the correct words to complete the email to department store employees.

To: Sales staff   From: Management team   Date: November 20

Thanks to all of you for agreeing to work longer hours this Friday during our one-day pre-holiday sale. I want to go over some special instructions for one-day sales. **Any / Some** of you are already familiar with these, and **others / another** are not, but I'd like everyone to go over them carefully.

When the store opens at 6:00 a.m., customers will already be lined up outside. **Some / Any** will be impatient. Do not slow down traffic by standing in the main aisles.

Some / Another popular items will be "flying off the shelves." If you notice the stock of an item running low, call the stockroom to bring up more merchandise. This way, any potential conflict between customers can be avoided.

Customers may have to wait in line for our most popular sales items. **Any / Some** customer that tries to cut in line should be directed to the end of the line. **Any / Some** serious arguments that break out should be handled by security.

We will run out of the most popular merchandise before noon. Try to persuade disappointed customers to consider **other / another** similar items so that they still purchase something.

Any / Some salesperson working at the cash registers needs to be aware of how many people are waiting in line. If **some / any** line is longer than five people, you need to notify management so that **another / other** register can be opened right away.

I know **some / any** of you have complained in the past about the loud music we play all day. Please keep in mind that our research indicates that this type of music encourages people to buy.

Finally, as always, **some / any** customers will be polite and courteous and **other / others** customers will not. Remain calm and treat people with courtesy no matter how they act toward you.

Thank you again for your dedication and hard work!

B Complete the conversation between two salespeople with the words in the box.

another	any	some	some other	other	others

A Wow! What a day! I'm really exhausted! _____¹ of the customers were nice, but _____² were kind of rude.

B Actually, _____³ were totally rude. I mean, one of my customers was reaching for a laptop he wanted when _____⁴ customer came up and grabbed it. I had to call security.

A Well, one of my customers got into a fight with some _____⁵ customers who saw him cutting in line for wide-screen TVs.

B Well, thank goodness for the security guards. It seemed like they were pretty tough on _____⁶ customer who got into a fight.

A The music didn't help. _____⁷ people liked it, but it was driving _____⁸ crazy.

B You can say that again. We should suggest _____⁹ kind of music for next year.

A I don't know. _____¹⁰ suggestion I make to that new manager is ignored.

B Well, if the _____¹¹ one is working tomorrow, you know, the nice one, tell her.

About you **C** Answer the questions with information that is true for you.

1. Do you like to shop in stores when there are big sales? Why or why not?

_____

2. What kinds of things have you bought on sale? Have you found any good bargains?

_____

Lesson C Conversation strategies

A Complete the conversation with the questions in the box.

> But aren't things changing?
> Couldn't that be the reason for the gap?
> So, it really isn't fair, is it?
>
> So, that's a good thing, isn't it?
> So, shouldn't they earn just as much as men?
> That's still a big gap, don't you think?

A You know, it's really annoying that women still don't earn as much as men.

B Yeah, but the wage gap has closed a lot over the last 50 years. Women earn more now than they ever did before. _____1

A I guess it is, and things *are* better than they used to be, but women still only earn about 77 percent of what men earn. _____2

B Yeah, I guess that is still a significant difference. But more men finish college than women. _____3

A No, actually, I read that more women get college degrees than men. What's more, women with the very same education and working in the same jobs still earn less than men. _____4

B No, it's not, I agree. There's still some inequality. _____5
I just read that more women are becoming the primary wage earners in their families.

A Right. But think about it. Women now have more and more responsibility for supporting their families. _____6

B Rewrite the questions in the conversation in Exercise A. Change the tag questions to negative questions and change the negative questions to tag questions.

1. _____
2. _____
3. _____
4. _____
5. _____
6. _____

C Rewrite each of Speaker A's statements as a negative question and as a tag question. Add *granted* to the correct places in Speaker B's replies. Add commas where necessary.

1. *A* The government needs more money for infrastructure projects. So people need to pay higher taxes.

   Doesn't the government need more money for infrastructure projects?

   The government needs more money for infrastructure projects, doesn't it?

   B _____ the government needs more tax revenue, but _____ corporations also benefit from government projects, so they should pay higher taxes, too.

2. *A* Companies have a responsibility to ensure that they don't cause any environmental damage.

   _____

   _____

   B Well, _____ the government really needs to pass more legislation to protect the environment, but companies should take more responsibility, _____ .

3. *A* It's really unfair when a company doesn't have equal numbers of male and female managers.

   _____

   _____

   B Well, _____ it is unfair. But it can be difficult to fix that.

Lesson D Reading Natural disasters and businesses

A Prepare Write down three things that a business would want to protect in the event of a natural disaster. Then scan the article to see if your ideas are mentioned.

1. _____   2. _____   3. _____

B Read for main ideas Read the article. What important items should a business protect from a natural disaster?

Protect Business Records and Inventory

PROTECTING YOUR PROPERTY FROM NATURAL HAZARDS

1   Most businesses keep on-site records and files (both hardcopy and electronic) that are essential to normal operations. Some businesses also store raw materials and product inventory. The loss of essential records, files, and other materials during a disaster is commonplace and can not only add to your damage costs but also delay your return to normal operations. The longer your business is not operating, the more likely you are to lose customers permanently to your competitors.

2   To reduce your vulnerability, determine which records, files, and materials are most important; consider their vulnerability to damage during different types of disasters (such as floods, hurricanes, and earthquakes) and take steps to protect them, including the following:
- Raising computers above the flood level and moving them away from large windows
- Moving heavy and fragile objects to low shelves
- Storing vital documents (plans, legal papers, etc.) in a secure off-site location
- Regularly backing up vital electronic files (such as billing and payroll records and customer lists) and storing backup copies in a secure off-site location
- Securing equipment that could move or fall during an earthquake
- Prior to hurricanes, cover or protect vital documents and electrical equipment from potential wind driven rain, which may breech the building envelope through windows, doors, or roof systems.

TIPS

3   Keep these points in mind when protecting your business records and inventory:
- Make sure you are aware of the details of your flood insurance and other hazard insurance policies, specifically which items and contents are covered and under what conditions. For example, if you have a home business, you may need two flood insurance policies, a home policy and a separate business policy, depending on the percentage of the total square footage of your house that is devoted to business use. Check with your insurance agent if you have questions about any of your policies.
- When you identify equipment susceptible to damage, consider the location of the equipment. For example, equipment near a hot water tank or pipes could be damaged if the pipes burst during an earthquake, and equipment near large windows could be damaged during hurricanes.
- Assign disaster mitigation duties to your employees. For example, some employees could be responsible for securing storage bins and others for backing up computer files and delivering copies to a secure location.
- You may want to consider having other offices of your company or a contractor perform some administrative duties, such as maintaining payroll records or providing customer service.
- Estimate the cost of repairing or replacing each essential piece of equipment in your business. Your estimates will help you assess your vulnerability and focus your efforts.
- For both insurance and tax purposes, you should maintain written and photographic inventories of all important materials and equipment. The inventory should be stored in a safety deposit box or other secure location.
- Periodically evaluate the building envelope to make sure that wind and water are not able to penetrate the building. Do regular maintenance and repairs to maintain the strength of the building envelope.

SOURCE: U.S. Department of Homeland Security - FEMA

C **Check your understanding** Check (✔) the correct answer to each question.

1. The most serious consequence of not being prepared for a natural disaster is that . . .
   _____ a. your computer equipment may get damaged.
   _____ b. you may lose business.
   _____ c. you may lose your payroll records.
2. The suggestions are divided into two sections that outline . . .
   _____ a. things to do before an emergency and things to do after an emergency.
   _____ b. suggestions for business owners and suggestions for business employees.
   _____ c. how to protect the most important things and suggestions for other actions to take.
3. The article suggests that precautionary actions need to be taken . . .
   _____ a. once.
   _____ b. yearly.
   _____ c. regularly.

D **Read for inference** Why do you think the article suggests these actions? Match each suggestion with a probable reason.

1. Raise computers above flood level _____
2. Move heavy and fragile equipment to low shelves _____
3. Regularly back up electronic files _____
4. Hire a third party to maintain payroll records _____
5. Assign disaster mitigation duties to employees _____
6. Maintain photographic inventories of equipment _____
7. Consider the location of vulnerable equipment _____
8. Periodically evaluate and maintain the building envelope _____

a. so that wind and water don't enter the building.
b. so that your records will be in a secure location.
c. so that they don't fall and break.
d. so that you can file a claim with the insurance company.
e. so that electronic equipment does not suffer water damage.
f. so that you can move it to a safe place in preparation for a natural disaster.
g. so that there's a team ready to take action as soon as disaster strikes.
h. so that your company records are up to date

About you

E **React** Answer the questions about the article with your own ideas and opinions.

1. Which suggestions do you think would be the most useful for businesses in your city or region? Why?

   _____

   _____

2. Which of the suggestions do you think are most difficult for businesses to follow?

   _____

   _____

3. Which suggestions could you use to protect your own personal possessions in the case of a disaster?

   _____

   _____

Writing A report analyzing a problem

A **Complete the report with the expressions in the box. Then circle the correct modal verbs to complete the sentences.**

Another possible reason that	One reason for this
It may also be a result of	This is possibly because

It is now one year since we launched our company website, and the results have not been as good as we had hoped. A lot of potential customers visit the site, but they seem to leave before viewing any of the products that we offer. _____¹ may be the design of the website. The first page that people see is very confusing and **might / would** offer too many choices. As a result, customers **may / could** not take the time to figure out how to navigate to other parts of the site. We could solve this if we had a simpler design. _____² people leave the site so quickly **can / could** be that it isn't updated and refreshed often enough. Nothing puts customers off more than dead links and out-of-date information. We **could / might** plan to update the site on a weekly basis.

Another problem to address is that customers frequently do not complete the ordering process. _____³ it is difficult to find the button you need to click on in order to move to the next page. _____⁴ the complicated "check-out" page, where people have discovered that it **can / could** be difficult to make changes in the order. Customers tell us that problems like these **can / would** be frustrating and deter people from completing their order. This should be fixed as soon as possible, but in the meantime, we **could / may** list our phone number more prominently on the page. It will take some time to fix all of these problems, but it **can / would** be advisable to get started right away. Any changes we make **could / can** have an immediate impact on online sales of our products.

B **Rewrite the second sentences more formally with the expressions given in parentheses. Make any other necessary changes.**

1. Our website often scares people off. Maybe it's the very complicated design. (This may be a result of . . .)

   _____

2. Our customers often don't complete their orders. It's very confusing to go through the ordering process. (One reason for this might be . . .)

   _____

3. People get very frustrated on our website. Maybe it's because of all the dead links and out-of-date information. (A possible cause could be . . .)

   _____

C **Editing Correct the mistakes. One sentence is correct.**

1. If our website had a better design, people can navigate through it more easily.
2. People tell us that they are using our new website and they could find things more easily.
3. I just discovered a great website where you could order foods from all over the world.
4. Some news sites have so many pop-up ads that you could hardly read the articles.
5. One nice thing about the travel site I use is that you can get special discounts on flights.
6. There used to be a site where I can get discounts on designer clothing, but it's gone now.

D **Write a report on a problem that you feel needs attention at your school or place of work. Then check your report for errors.**

Listening extra Miscommunication in the workplace

A Which topics do you think would be interesting to learn about? Check (✔) the boxes. Can you think of other topics?

☐ Employee hostility   ☐ Face-to-face communication
☐ Lost productivity   ☐ Email correspondence
☐ Boss–employee relationships   ☐ Problems with the bottom line

B ⬇ Listen to a recording of a training course on workplace miscommunication. Check (✔) the main cause of miscommunication the trainer focuses on.

☐ a. Timing your message badly
☐ b. Using the wrong form of communication
☐ c. Not being a good enough observer
☐ d. Poor listening skills

C ⬇ Listen again. Circle the best options to complete the sentences.

1. According to the speaker, miscommunication is an issue in _____ .
   a. boss–employee relationships   b. knowing people too well   c. staff meetings

2. According to the trainer, the disadvantage of email is that you may not know if employees have _____ your message.
   a. responded to   b. understood   c. read

3. She says that email communication is inefficient because it often requires _____ .
   a. clarification   b. no feedback   c. a fast exchange of messages

4. She says that emails are inefficient because they _____ .
   a. aren't always read   b. take too long to write   c. lead to more emails

5. According to the trainer, bad news is best communicated _____ .
   a. in person   b. electronically   c. in a personal letter

6. Solutions to communication problems are covered in _____ of this program.
   a. the second part   b. every part   c. the last part

7. According to the lecturer, the first step in improving workplace communication is _____ .
   a. taking notes   b. observing behavior   c. doing homework on how to communicate

About you

D Answer the questions with your own ideas and opinions.

1. Which information in the talk was new or surprising to you? _____
   _____

2. Do you agree with the trainer that face-to-face communication is more effective than email? Why or why not? _____
   _____

3. Have you ever had a problem with miscommunication? What do you think might have caused it? _____
   _____

Now complete the *Unit 6 Progress chart* on page 99. Unit 6: Business studies **49**

Progress charts

Unit 1 Progress chart

Mark the boxes to rate your progress.
☑ I can do it.   ? I can do it, but have questions.   ! I need to review it.

I can . . .	To review, go back to these pages in the Student's Book.
☐ discuss literature, reading habits, and favorite authors.	12
☐ discuss the pros and cons of reading and writing blogs.	14–15
☐ use auxiliary verbs *to, one,* and *ones* to avoid repetition.	13
☐ use 12 idioms for remembering and understanding, like *It's beyond me.*	12
☐ use stressed auxiliary verbs (*do, does*) before main verbs to add emphasis.	14
☐ use *if so* to mean "if this is true" and *if not* to mean "if this is not true."	15
☐ stress auxiliaries for emphasis.	138
☐ write a book review; link adjectives with *yet, though, if, though, if not,* or *even.*	18

Unit 2 Progress chart

Mark the boxes to rate your progress.
☑ I can do it.   ? I can do it, but have questions.   ! I need to review it.

I can . . .	To review, go back to these pages in the Student's Book.
☐ discuss technology and the issue of privacy vs. security.	20
☐ evaluate the pros and cons of modern conveniences.	27
☐ add information to nouns with different types of expressions.	21
☐ use two-part conjunctions like *either . . . or* to combine ideas.	23
☐ use 12 compound adjectives like *high-speed* to describe technology.	22
☐ use adverbs like *predictably* to express what I predict or expect.	24
☐ say what is impossible with *can't / couldn't possibly.*	25
☐ use stress in noun phrases.	138
☐ write a report describing graphs, charts, and tables using expressions like *as can be seen in the graph,* etc.	28

Unit 3 Progress chart

Mark the boxes to rate your progress.
☑ I can do it.   ? I can do it, but have questions.   ! I need to review it.

I can . . .	To review, go back to these pages in the Student's Book.
☐ discuss social pressures, challenges, and other new experiences.	30, 32
☐ discuss gender differences in language.	37
☐ use participle clauses to link events and add information about time or reason.	31
☐ add emphasis with *so . . . that, such . . . that, even,* and *only.*	33
☐ use at least 12 expressions with *take* (*take advantage of, take credit for*).	32
☐ use *even so* and *even then* to introduce a contrasting idea.	35
☐ use stress in expressions of contrast.	139
☐ plan and write an evaluative report; use different ways to express results.	38

Unit 4 Progress chart

Mark the boxes to rate your progress. ☑ I can do it.　　☑ I can do it, but have questions.　　⚠ I need to review it. I can . . .	To review, go back to these pages in the Student's Book.
☐ discuss the natural world, landscapes, and animal behavior and habitats.	42, 44
☐ consider the impact that humans have on nature.	47
☐ use future perfect forms to talk about the past in the future.	43
☐ use prepositional expressions like *as a result of* to combine ideas.	45
☐ use at least 12 expressions to describe the behavior of wildlife (*hibernate, predator*).	42
☐ use expressions like *What's more* to add and focus on new ideas.	46
☐ use *in any case* and *in any event* to strengthen arguments and reach conclusions.	47
☐ use stress in adding expressions: adding information.	139
☐ write a persuasive essay using academic prepositions (*upon, within,* etc.) and *one* for general statements.	50

Unit 5 Progress chart

Mark the boxes to rate your progress. ☑ I can do it.　　☑ I can do it, but have questions.　　⚠ I need to review it. I can . . .	To review, go back to these pages in the Student's Book.
☐ discuss the pros and cons of research, inventions, and innovations.	52, 54
☐ evaluate the motivation of people who are driven to perform dangerous feats.	54
☐ use adverbs with continuous and perfect forms of the passive.	53
☐ use past modals with passive forms.	55
☐ use at least 12 formal adjectives like *obsolete, portable*, adjectives into nouns (*convenient—convenience; easy—ease*).	52
☐ use expressions like *Let's put it this way* to make a point.	56
☐ use expressions like *Maybe (not), Absolutely (not), Not necessarily* in responses.	57
☐ use primary and secondary stress in expressions.	140
☐ write an opinion essay; use *it*-clauses + passive to say what people think.	60

Unit 6 Progress chart

Mark the boxes to rate your progress. ☑ I can do it.　　☑ I can do it, but have questions.　　⚠ I need to review it. I can . . .	To review, go back to these pages in the Student's Book.
☐ discuss business and retail; consider motivations behind shopping habits.	62, 64
☐ evaluate the benefits of online and instore shopping big and small business.	65
☐ use relative clauses that begin with pronouns or prepositions.	63
☐ use *some, any, other, others,* and *another* to refer to people and things.	65
☐ use at least 12 verbs that mean *attract* and *deter* (*entice, discourage*).	64
☐ use negative and tag questions to persuade others of your point of view.	66
☐ use *granted* to concede points.	67
☐ reduce prepositions in relative clauses.	140
☐ write a report using modal verbs to avoid being too assertive and to make recommendations.	70

Author acknowledgements

The authors would like to thank everyone who contributed material and ideas to this workbook: Guy de Villiers, Deborah Gordon, Natasha Isadora, Therese Naber, Allison Ramage, and Mary Vaughn.

Photography credits

3 Exactostock/SuperStock; *(background)* Lichtmeister/Shutterstock **5** Tetra Images/SuperStock **6** Brian Cahn/ZUMA Press/Corbis; *(background)* Microstock Man/Shutterstock **9** Nickolay Vinokurov/Shutterstock **10** DNY59/ iStockphoto **11** *(top)* Michael DeLeon/iStockphoto; *(bottom)* Duncan Walker/iStockphoto; *(background)* Ersler Dmitry/ Shutterstock **12** PR NEWSWIRE/AP Images **13** Mik Lav/Shutterstock **17** dwphotos/Shutterstock **18** *(left to right)* Andrew Rich/iStockphoto; Darren Mower/iStockphoto; zhang bo/iStockphoto **19** Skip Odonnell/iStockphoto **20** Neustockimages/iStockphoto **22** Don Bayley/iStockphoto **25** DigitalVision/Getty Images **26** *(left to right)* Don Wilkie/iStockphoto; Willie Manalo/iStockphoto **27** *(top to bottom)* James E. Seward/Shutterstock; jo Crebbin/ Shutterstock **28** Jim Parkin/iStockphoto **30** Pixtal/SuperStock **33** *(left to right)* J & C Sohns/Tier und Naturfotografie/ SuperStock; Juniors/SuperStock **34** Tim Boryer/iStockphoto **35** UNIMEDIA/SIPA/Newscom; *(background)* Adrian Grosu/Shutterstock **36** Rob Griffith/AP Photo; *(background)* Willyam Bradberry/Shutterstock **38** Pgiam/ iStockphoto **39** *(top to bottom)* UIG via Getty Images; imagebroker.net/SuperStock **41** David J. Green - technology/ Alamy **43** slobo/iStockphoto **46** Henrik Sorensen/Getty Images; *(background)* isoga/Shutterstock **49** Blend Images/ SuperStock

Text credits

The authors and publishers are grateful for permission to reprint the following items:

6 "Poetry Slam - General FAQ" from www.poetryslam.com. Reprinted by permission. **14** "E-books spur reading among Americans, survey shows" by Amy Gahran, www.cnn.com, April 5, 2012. Reprinted by permission. **22** "The changing language of the internet" from www.writemysite.co.uk. Reprinted by permission. **30** "Toads able to detect earthquake days beforehand, says study" by Alok Jha, www.guardian.co.uk, March 31, 2010. Reprinted by permission. **38** "The Invention of Paper" from Wisconsin Paper Council. **46** "Protect Business Records and Inventory" from www.fema.gov. Reprinted by permission.

Corpus

Development of this publication has made use of the Cambridge English Corpus (CEC). The CEC is a computer database of contemporary spoken and written English, which currently stands at over one billion words. It includes British English, American English and other varieties of English. It also includes the Cambridge Learner Corpus, developed in collaboration with the University of Cambridge ESOL Examinations. Cambridge University Press has built up the CEC to provide evidence about language use that helps to produce better language teaching materials.